SOCIOLOGY OF EDUCATION SERIES
Aaron M. Pallas, Series Editor

Advisory Board: Sanford Dornbusch, Adam Gamoran, Annette Lareau,
Mary Metz, Gary Natriello

FROM THE SERIES EDITOR

Connoisseurs of fine foods know Modena, Italy, to be the home of balsamic vinegar, one of the world's great condiments. The finest grades are aged in wood for decades, resulting in a thick syrup dramatically different from the industrial-grade varieties commonly available. The artisans who create this prized vinegar have a keen appreciation of the importance of time.

Time is also at the center of William Corsaro and Luisa Molinari's remarkable longitudinal ethnography, *I Compagni*. The study is situated in Modena, which adjoins Reggio Emilia, justly celebrated for its approach to preschool education. Corsaro and Molinari trace the experiences of a group of Modena children as they move from preschool into the elementary school years. Each school year poses new developmental challenges, and Corsaro and Molinari capitalize on knowledge of the children's prior school experiences as they engage with new school routines and practices. The central analytic concept is the priming event, a collective participatory experience by which children are able to anticipate and reflect on coming changes in their lives at school. Priming events are not serendipitous; rather, they are woven into the fabric of school and family life in Modena, ensuring that children undergo transitions not in isolation from one another, but instead as members of a community with shared experience. The result is an enviable structure of transitions free of some of the rough edges that plague less planful systems of schooling.

The pairing of William Corsaro and Luisa Molinari is particularly powerful. Corsaro brings a keen interpretive eye to every facet of young children's lives. An American man in his 40s during the study, he became a true participant observer, which delighted the young Italian children who befriended him. Molinari, an Italian psychologist who studies children and adolescents, offers a deep understanding of the regional and national context for school transitions in Modena.

A fine balsamic vinegar is both tart and sweet, but never cloying. So too with *I Compagni*. Although the children chronicled by Corsaro and Molinari are utterly charming, the text retains a precise analytic rigor. Much as a single drop of an artisanal balsamic can enhance an entire meal, this volume extends and deepens our understanding of the sociology of childhood and of primary schooling.

Aaron M. Pallas

I Compagni

Understanding Children's Transition from Preschool to Elementary School

WILLIAM A. CORSARO
LUISA MOLINARI

CAROLYN POPE EDWARDS
FOREWORD

TEACHERS COLLEGE PRESS

Teachers College, Columbia University
New York and London

Published by Teachers College Press, 1234 Amsterdam Avenue, New York, NY 10027

We are grateful to the American Sociological Association to reprint some of the material contained in this book:

Parts of Chapters 3, 4, and 7 first appeared in William A. Corsaro and Luisa Molinari, "Priming events and Italian children's transition form preschool to elementary school: Representations and action," *Social Psychology Quarterly*, 63, 16–33, 2000 and William A. Corsaro, Luisa Molinari, Kathryn Gold Hadley, and Heather Sugioka, "Keeping and making friends: Italian children's transition from preschool to elementary school," in *Social Psychology Quarterly*, 66, 272–292, 2003.

Library of Congress Cataloging-in-Publication Data

Corsaro, William A.
  I compagni : understanding children's transition from preschool to elementary school / William A. Corsaro, Luisa Molinari ; foreword by Carolyn Edwards.
    p. cm. — (Sociology of education series)
  Includes bibliographical references and index.
  ISBN 0-8077-4619-3 (cloth) — ISBN 0-8077-4618-5 (pbk.)
  1. Socialization—Italy—Modena—Case studies.   2. Readiness for school—Italy—Modena—Case studies.   3. Education, Preschool—Italy—Modena—Case studies.   4. Education, Elementary—Social aspects—Italy—Modena—Case studies.
  I. Molinari, Luisa.   II. Title.   III. Sociology of education series (New York, N.Y.)
  LC192.4.C67 2005
  372'.945'42—dc22   2005044010

ISBN 0-8077-4618-5 (paper)
ISBN 0-8077-4619-3 (cloth)

Printed on acid-free paper

Manufactured in the United States of America

12 11 10 09 08 07 06 05   8 7 6 5 4 3 2 1

To *i compagni*, the wonderful children of Modena
who shared their lives with us.

Contents

Part III   STUDYING AND DEEPENING FRIENDSHIPS AT GIACOMO PUCCINI ELEMENTARY SCHOOL

Foreword

This book will be welcome to readers because it tells a full and important story about the social lives of young children as they grow from young preschoolers to preadolescents in middle school. That story is interesting in its own right, and also because it complements the literature on experiences for children in other high-quality Italian public early care and education systems. Here the focus is Modena, a city nearby to Reggio Emilia and part of the same northern region, Emilia Romagna, known to the world for its innovations in early education and progressive public administration. As in Reggio Emilia, virtually all children in Modena aged 3 to 5 years old attend full-day public or private preschool of some kind, based on the families' values that this is a beneficial thing for young children.

The value of an educational case study such as *I Compagni* lies in the ways it invites consideration of relationships between education and socialization and the historical and cultural surroundings that precondition them. North Americans have access to parallel well-rounded information for a few Italian cities, notably Reggio Emilia, Pistoia, and Milan, so it is useful to have Modena join the set. Modena has the noteworthy feature that Loris Malaguzzi, who founded the early childhood system in Reggio Emilia and was its leading theoretician, also played a key role in the early days of Modena's early childhood system. Yet Modena has its own history and evolving political context, and educators and citizens there have made some similar but also some different choices from Reggio Emilia in cultivating quality. For example, Modena features a different use of subject-matter specialists to extend the work of classroom teachers, and there is strong coordination between preschool and elementary systems. Through *I Compagni* we gain a glimpse into the Italian elementary school experience and widen our understanding of the dialogues, debates, and exchanges that have provided so much vitality to the historical development of early education in Italy. Put together with other studies, this book helps us to more fully comprehend what Italians mean when they speak of a *culture of childhood*, that is, a politically forged set of shared community values favorable to the interests and rights of young children (Gandini & Edwards, 2001; Susanna Mantovani's interview in Edwards, Gandini, Peon-Casanova, & Danielson, 2003).

Previous studies of Italian systems by early childhood educators such as myself have tended to focus on topics such as education as relationships, curriculum, environments, organizational and educational strategies, and how *progettazione* (projected curriculum constructed through documentation) yields an educational and formative experience for children, families, and the educators themselves. This book, instead, offers analyses and interpretations of the meaning of how children and their parents experience the group life and daily routines inside their schools and preschools, and ideas about how participating in this solidarity helps children grow and develop as individuals over time. The transitions between each level of formal education are studied to learn how the children negotiate the change from one stage of childhood to the next. Moreover, children's sense of belonging is promoted not only inside the school but also outside, through children's exuberant inclusion in town civic life, giving them pride and participatory power at a young age.

The authors, William Corsaro and Luisa Molinari, are a team of cultural outsider and cultural insider that is effective in doing ethnography because the questions and reframing observations of the outsider provoke, but are restrained and corrected by, the knowledge and interpretations of the insider. Corsaro is known as a leading authority on the sociology of childhood, and Molinari plays the role of cultural broker and educational expert, while being the mother of three children in Modena. Corsaro actually did the daily data collection for this longitudinal ethnography, and readers will realize right away why the children, parents, and teachers responded so positively to comical "Big Bill" and let him into their lives. The many stories and episodes in the book are not just intended to liven it up, however. They serve as both the substance of rich description and as memorable instances for the theoretical framework. Aspects of this framework offer fresh insight on the sources and substance of high quality in the Italian system. In particular, the notions of *priming events* and *rites of passage* are used to explain what makes for smooth transitions. I found the notion of priming events (projective social representations of the future, embedded in daily routines) to increase my appreciation of the educational value for children of long-term projects, class trips, and celebrations—highlights of the year for Modena preschool children and families.

In their final chapters, the authors step back and reflect on what their study suggests about creating and sustaining a high-quality system in ways that are line with others' comparative conclusions. In their view, the U.S. preschool system is fragmented, underfunded, and squeezed in a political vice compared to Italy's, where the high quality of preschool experience puts Italian children at an advantage over American children in making the transition to elementary school. An important ingredient is the continuity of the same group of children and teachers staying together for several years, and this may be especially beneficial for immigrant children or those with special needs. This book is valuable because empirical evidence is provided for the value of continuity—qualitative data, to be sure, yet this is different from arguing by anecdote because the observational data were collected systematically and with a constant search for "negative cases," or instances that went in the opposite direction of the general trends of the data.

The Italian situation also has its problems, however. Recent changes in Italian law make it possible for school systems to allow certain 5-year-old children (those born in the first months of the year) to skip their third year of preschool and go directly to elementary. Furthermore, other aspects of current reforms involve changes in the length of the school day and reduce the total number of school hours. These changes, very much debated throughout Italy today, are of concern to Corsaro and Molinari because they may undercut peer solidarity and mutual support in preschool and elementary in ways that the Italians themselves (who take childhood peer culture for granted) have not fully realized or thought through. Watching this issue unfold and play out in the next few years should be important and interesting for American educators and policymakers.

No book can answer all one's questions or provide all the evidence one might desire. In the end, the conclusions of this book are limited by the sample and analytic techniques, as are all research studies. Yet as you read along, you should find some vivid examples for use in discussion of several enduring topics of equal interest to researchers and practicing teachers: the waxing and waning of gender segregation over time (through the development of close relationships); teacher intervention in children's conflicts; early skills in verbal debate and discussion; children's attachment to teachers; sibling support; promoting parental involvement and psychological capital; preliteracy and literacy instruction, ways of doing story-reading and integrating curriculum; children's fears and worries; and children's needs for disorder as well as order.

—*Carolyn Pope Edwards*

REFERENCES

Edwards, C. P., Gandini, L., Peon-Casanova, L., & Danielson, J. (2003). *Bambini: early child care and education in Pistoia, Italy, a child-friendly city.* (Video). New York: Teachers College Press.

Gandini, L., & Edwards, C. P. (Eds.) (2001). *Bambini: The Italian approach to infant/toddler care.* New York: Teachers College Press.

Preface

When seeking a model for high-quality preschool programs, many early education researchers and teachers in North America have looked to Italy, and most especially the city of Reggio Emilia. Undoubtedly, Reggio Emilia has some of the best preschools in the world in terms of structure, administration, teacher training, curriculum, teacher-child relations, and parental involvement. The implications for schools in the United States has been well documented (Cadwell, 1997, 2003; Edwards, Gandini, & Forman, 1993; Giudici, Rinaldi, & Krechevsky, 2001; Helm & Katz, 2001; New, 1997). Yet, quality preschool education is a staple throughout the Emilia-Romagna region of Italy; and interest in and development of excellent preschool programs have spread throughout northern and central Italy. Important inroads in quality programs have been forged in southern Italy as well. Over 96 percent of Italian 3–5-year-olds attend government-supported preschool in Italy. This figure makes it clear that Italian parents trust and support their country's system of preschool education.

BEYOND REGGIO EMILIA

In this book we expand upon the earlier literature on preschool in Italy in two ways. First, we investigate a high-quality preschool program in another city of Emilia-Romagna, Modena, which shares much of the history of commitment to quality, community-based preschools that exists in Reggio Emilia. In doing so, we want to dispel the notion that Reggio Emilia is unique, and stress the long history of quality early education throughout the Emilia-Romagna region. Our investigation adds an important case study to the mix of work on Italian early education.

Second, our study of early education in Modena does not stop with preschool, but examines the transition from preschools to elementary schools in Modena, highlighting elements of continuity and discontinuity between the two school systems. To capture this process of transition, we follow a group of preschool children in their entry into first grade and progress through elementary school. While we now know a great deal about preschool in Italy (and especially Reggio Emilia) and also more recently have studies of the

Italian approach to infant and toddler care (Gandini & Edwards, 2001), there is relatively little information in the United States on elementary schools in Italy.

What happens when Italian children move on from preschool to elementary school? What is the nature of this important transition? How coordinated are the two levels of schooling regarding their organization, structure, and general educational philosophy? Not all of these questions can be answered in a single case study. However, this book is important because it examines the issue of how children are prepared or primed for their transition from the *scuola dell'infanzia* to state-run *scuola elementare*. Although there has been so much attention on the high quality of the Reggio approach, there has been little research that addresses this issue of transition in children's educational, social, and cultural lives as they move forward in the Italian educational system. One of our main goals is to document the details and complexity of this transition process.

In addition to documenting a rich school culture in line with the Reggio Emilia approach, this book also documents in great detail the peer culture that developed in two particular schools that have all the features of quality education. We demonstrate how children learn and develop, but also how they appropriate information from the adult culture in the school to create and participate in their own peer culture. This contribution is important because most of the prior work on early education in Reggio Emila has paid rather scant attention to peer culture.

WHY MODENA?

There are several reasons why we selected Modena for our case study. First, Modena is representative of the many other cities in the Emilia-Romagna region that have high-quality communal preschools. As noted earlier, we know little about the quality of preschools throughout the region except for Reggio Emilia. Second, Modena has a clear history of high-quality and innovative elementary school programs. As we describe in the appendix, there are important elements of cooperation between the elementary schools' programs and the larger civic community in Modena. Third, Modena is a city with a progressive left-wing government that has strong civic pride and significant labor union activism. In fact, Modena's highly organized teachers' union had forged close relations with the city's political leaders. Finally, to some degree our choice of Modena schools was for convenience because the directors and teachers at the preschool and elementary school were open to and interested in our study, most especially our goal of following the children from preschool operated by the city (or commune) to the state-run elementary school.

A UNIQUE COLLABORATION

A final key strength of this book is the collaborative nature of our re-search. We had worked together on several earlier studies and pooled our data on observations in an Italian *asilo nido* for 2-year-olds and younger (Luisa Molinari) and a *scuola dell'infanzia* (Bill Corsaro) in Bologna to study the emergence and extension of peer culture among Italian preschool children (Corsaro & Molinari, 1990; Molinari & Corsaro, 1994). In the present study, Luisa negotiated field entry with the director of the preschool, the elementary school director, and the preschool and first-grade teachers. Together we presented our research aims and described the study to parents and later presented interim reports of initial findings to the teachers, parents, and interested members of the community. Luisa's knowledge of the preschool and elementary school systems in Modena (she was the mother of three young children who were at various points in these systems at the time of the research) was essential in developing initial rapport with the gatekeepers and in navigating through the bureaucracy of early education in Italy.

An obvious question arises here: why didn't Luisa, who was a native to the culture and region of Italy, conduct the ethnographic research? Aside from the fact that Bill had a great deal more experience as an ethnographer of young children, there is another—perhaps more important—reason for our collaboration in this way. The ethnographer's acceptance into the world of children is especially difficult because of obvious differences between adults and children in terms of cognitive and communicative maturity, power, and physical size. In Bill's earlier work in Bologna his lack of fluency in Italian (he was in fact about at the first-grade level) led the children to see him as an "adult incompetent" (Corsaro, 2003). This incompetence helped Bill overcome many of the obstacles to becoming accepted and drawn into children's everyday lives in Bologna (Corsaro, 1996). It was also a positive factor in this case study. In fact, we would argue that one of the strengths of cross-cultural ethnographies of children is that the foreign ethnographer is often seen as a less threatening adult by children and youth. Thus, the ethnographer not only is more easily accepted into the children's lives, but is able to gain the children's perspective on their participation in both the adult world and their own peer cultures (see also Berentzen, 1995; Wulff, 1988).

In addition to the joint accomplishment of practical research tasks, Bill and Luisa met twice a week to reflect on and discuss the ongoing research process. These meetings provided opportunities for evaluating Bill's reactions to events he observed in the field, discussing ideas about data collection strategies, analyzing observational and interview data, and generating and discussing initial interpretations. Our collaboration on this comparative, longitudinal study is unique in many ways. Overall, we found that our different cultural backgrounds and research experience enriched the quality of this collaborative ethnography (see Corsaro & Molinari, 2000a).

OVERVIEW OF THE BOOK

This book has four parts. In Part I we introduce the city of Modena and its schools, especially our field sites. We also present our theoretical framework for understanding children's early life transitions. In Part II we turn to our analysis of the school and peer cultures of the preschool we studied. Here we describe basic routine practices, activities, and events in the school and peer cultures, and especially note how these processes prepare or prime children for their coming transition to elementary school. Part II also contains our analysis of interviews with children, parents, and teachers regarding their perceptions of the coming transition at the end of the preschool year.

In Part III we first examine the school and peer cultures as they develop in the first grade of elementary school. Here we focus on the overall quality of the children's transition and adjustments to the academic and social demands of elementary school. Next, we analyze interview data in which the teachers, children, and parents reflect on the transition process at the completion of first grade. Finally, we describe the school features and peer cultures in Grades 2 through 5 and consider priming events that prepare the children for their transition to middle school.

In Part IV we present our conclusions and discuss their contributions to theoretical work on children's early life transitions. We also consider the implications of our findings for early education policy and practice in Italy and the United States.

Acknowledgments

The heart of this book is longitudinal ethnography. Doing longitudinal ethnography is exciting and inspirational; and when carried out in a deeply collaborative way, as in this study, it is an immensely rewarding personal experience. The title of the book, *I Compagni* (the companions), has multiple meanings. Primarily, it refers to the children's strong communal relations in preschool and elementary school, but it also signifies our strong personal relations with the children over the 6 years of the study. In addition, it captures our own collaborative experience which was well established before this project, but reached a new level of deep mutual respect, interdependence, and trust in carrying out our research and writing this book.

We have many wonderful people in Modena to thank for making this book possible. We want to acknowledge first the coordinator of the preschool and the two directors of the elementary school who gave us both access to and support in their schools. They could have easily said no and avoided any possible problems our study may have caused, but they welcomed us into the schools, showed great interest in our project, and were supportive throughout. Second, we express our sincere gratitude to the preschool and elementary school teachers in Modena who opened up their classrooms to us, embraced us into the rich cultures of these classrooms, agreed to multiple interviews, made insightful suggestions, and became dear friends. We especially want to thank Lucia Selmi, coordinator of *scuole dell'infanzia* Comune di Modena, and Gianna Ferretti, an elementary school teacher, with assistance in preparing the appendix. Third, we thank all of the parents of the children who participated in the study; they showed a genuine interest in our work and made us feel at home in the many civic activities that typified their strong involvement in their children's early schooling. We are especially grateful to that small group of eight families who agreed to multiple interviews, welcomed us repeatedly into their homes, and shared with us their concerns, support, and love for their children; we came to feel like we were part of their families and developed long-lasting and deep friendships.

Last but certainly not least, we thank the many children who participated in this study from the original 21 in preschool to the 80 plus in elementary school. We were given a unique opportunity to grow up with these children, to be their companions and friends as they made major steps in their educational experiences and their peer relations. The children often told us they felt special because we stayed with them, shared in their lives, and considered them true friends. For our part, we felt not only special, but honored, and often deeply touched by the children's interest in our project, our families, and our lives. Adults can only live their childhoods once, but this study taught us that it is possible for adults to share and participate in children's childhoods. We will remember and cherish our experiences with these children of Modena all of our lives.

We also want to thank colleagues who worked with us in data collection and analysis on this project and the composition of interpretive narratives that make up this book. They include Hilary Aydt, Kathryn Hadley, Elizabeth Nelson, Katherine Brown Rosier, Heather Sugioka, and especially Silvia Zetti.

Research reported on in this book was supported by the Spencer Foundation and Indiana University, Bloomington. We want to thank Susan Liddicoat at Teachers College Press for being supportive throughout this project and nourishing the production of this book. We are also thankful to two anonymous reviewers for their insightful comments and suggestions on early draft chapters, which we feel contributed greatly to the final product.

Finally, we want to thank our families (Vickie Renfrow and Veronica Corsaro, and Hermod, Francesco, Edoardo, and Carlotta Allertsen) for their support, patience, and love.

PART I

Community, Priming, and Transition

CHAPTER I

Exploring the Context:
Early Education in Modena, Italy

We began our observations in a Modena preschool in early February about a week before *Carnevale*—a big celebration for the kids that occurred over 2 days. All the children, teachers, and staff dressed in costumes, and there was singing, dancing, and many good things to eat. Among the highlights of the first day of the celebration was a skit put on by the teachers, "The Lambs and the Wolf," during which the children clapped and cheered for their teachers' performances. Later the children were entertained by a magician who involved many of the children in his repertoire of fascinating tricks. On the second day, the teachers of the 5-year-olds that we studied now dressed as Pinocchio and Geppetto and gave a performance for all the kids in which Geppetto manipulated the puppet, Pinocchio, to perform many entertaining dances and stunts. Afterwards there was eating, singing, dancing, and throwing streamers. It was all great fun.

During the school celebration several children asked Bill if he was going to the celebration of *Carnevale* in Piazza Grande in the heart of the city. Bill said that he was and he attended the festivities with his 8-year-old daughter. There was a large crowd of over a thousand people at the event, including many of the kids from the preschool with their parents, grandparents, siblings, and classmates. The children were dressed in the costumes they had worn at school, and they had a great time running, throwing streamers, listening to music, and buying a variety of treats from vendors. This was one of many events in the city that were centered around children and were coordinated with activities in preschools and elementary schools.

THE LOCAL CONTEXT

Modena, a prosperous city of around 185,000 inhabitants, is located in the flat plane of two tributaries of the Po River in the Emilia-Romagna region of northern Italy. The wider province of Modena (645,000 inhabitants) also contains several smaller cities and fertile agricultural areas with the picturesque peaks of the Apennines visible in the southwest on clear days and a 45-minute drive from the city center. The province of Modena has one of the highest per capita incomes of Italy and rivals many of the more prosperous cities of similar size in Europe. With a number of thriving industries in food production (the famous balsamic vinegar), automobile manufacturing (the well-known Ferrari plant), ceramic tile and related products, and textiles, the province has one of the highest employment rates in Italy. Over 60 percent of women are in the workforce.

Modena has a rich cultural history with impressive architecture, most notably its main cathedral and bell tower, which are considered among the greatest masterpieces of the European Romanesque style. Its beautiful city center features narrow streets, many covered by ornate arcades like the larger city of Bologna to the south. A politically progressive city with a highly developed public transportation system and many parks and gardens, Modena has a high level of civic pride and participation. As mentioned earlier, a remarkable characteristic of Modena's civil society is its attention and investment in its children at both preschool and elementary school levels. A detailed account of the history, structure, and educational philosophy of preschool and elementary school education in Italy, and more specifically in Modena, is provided in the appendix.

A great deal has been written about the high quality of preschool education in Italy, especially in Emilia-Romagna. One of the central goals of this book is the documentation of children's transition from a high-quality preschool to a state-run elementary school, something that has been given little attention in the literature on Italian early education. The two schools we selected for study were representative of preschools and elementary schools in Modena in terms of the size and structure of the schools, curricula, resources, and the background of the students.

The *scuola dell'infanzia* (or preschool) we selected and call Giuseppe Verdi was made up of four classes with one 3- and one 4-year-old group and two 5-year-old groups. There were around 20 to 24 children in each class with two teachers plus additional teachers to work with any children who had special needs. In the class of 5-year-olds we studied there were 21 children and two teachers plus one part-time teacher who worked with one of the children who had special needs. Of the 21 children two (a boy who had returned to North Africa for most of the year and a girl who was absent until the last few weeks of school) were minor participants in our research. Among the remaining 19 children, one boy was mildly autistic and thus had somewhat limited participation in the peer culture. There was one immigrant child who was fluent in Italian and an active participant in the school and peer culture. (See Figure 1.1 for a list of the children in this class and the nature

Figure 1.1. Children in the 5-Year-Old Class at Giuseppe Verdi Preschool

Name	Made Transition to Giacomo Puccini Elementary School?	Participated in Interviews?
Alessio	No	No
Angelo	No	No
Carlotta	Yes to *Prima D*	Yes
Daniele	No	No
Elisa	Yes to *Prima B*	Yes
Federica	Yes to *Prima B*	No
Irene	Yes to *Prima D*	Yes
Lorenzo	No	No
Luciano	Yes to *Prima C*	Yes
Marina	Yes to *Prima A*	No
Mario	Yes to *Prima A*	No
Michela	Yes to *Prima A*	No
Michele	Yes to *Prima C*	No
Renato	Yes to *Prima B*	Yes
Sandra	Yes to *Prima D*	No
Sofia	Yes to *Prima A*	Yes
Sonia	Yes to *Prima B*	Yes
Stefania	Yes to *Prima C*	Yes
Valerio	Yes to *Prima D*	No
Viola	No	No
Viviana	Yes to *Prima A*	No

of their participation throughout the study.) The two teachers—Giovanna and Carla—had worked together for about 12 years at Giuseppe Verdi and had been preschool teachers for more than 18 years.

Of the 21 children in this preschool class, 16 went on to the *scuola elementare* (or elementary school) we call Giacomo Puccini and joined one of the four first-grade classes: Prima A, B, C, or D. The elementary school consisted of Grades 1 through 5, and the children and one of their teachers stayed together for the entire 5 years of elementary school. Thus, the first-grade teachers we worked with had just finished with a group of fifth graders who were moving on to middle school, and the teachers were now beginning with a new group of first graders. There were four first-grade classes with around 20 children in each class. In this particular year there were about twice as many girls as boys. This demographic quirk had some bearing on the teachers' decisions regarding the makeup of the classes in an attempt to have as many boys in each class as possible. There was also an attempt to balance the classes in terms of children with special needs and in terms of age range, as some children were several months younger than others. In each of the four first-grade classes there were two head teachers, one teaching Italian and history and the other teaching math, science, and geography. There was also a teacher for children with special needs in two of the classes, and an English teacher for the children from Grades 3 through 5.

All of the head teachers of Italian remained with the same class of children for all 5 years of elementary school. These four teachers had a great deal of teaching experience at the time our study began in 1996: Arianna in Prima A, 16 years all at Giacomo Puccini; Letizia in Prima B, 20 years with 12 at Giacomo Puccini; Renata in Prima C, 28 years with 16 at Giacomo Puccini; and Giusi in Prima D, 20 years with 13 at Giacomo Puccini.

THE ITALIAN CONTEXT

At this point we need to compare briefly the nature and quality of preschool education in Modena with that in Reggio Emilia, which is widely known, documented, and studied (Cadwell, 2003; Edwards, Gandini, & Forman, 1993, 1998; Giudici, Rinaldi, & Krechevsky, 2001; New, 1997).

The first city-run *scuola dell'infanzia* in Reggio Emilia was established by Loris Malaguzzi and a group of parents in 1963. The establishment of the school can be seen as an edcuational landmark in that for "the first time in Italy, the people affirmed the right to establish a secular school for young children: a rightful and necessary break in the monopoly the Catholic church had hitherto exercised over children's early education" (Malaguzzi, 1998, p. 52). Then other secular schools were established, and the highly innovative structure and curriculum that became known as the Reggio Emilia approach to early education was developed. However, secular community schools with similar educational philosophies and curricula were developing beyond Reggio Emilia in other areas of the Emilia-Romagna region, especially in Modena and Bologna. Many of these schools were greatly influenced by Malaguzzi and as well as by the writings of Bologna-based Bruno Ciari (1961, 1972; see also Corsaro & Emiliani, 1992).

Ciari, Malaguzzi, and others participated in lively debates and created growing interest in preschool education throughout Italy, but especially in the North (Edwards, Gandini, & Forman, 1998). Again, while it is fair to say that Reggio Emilia led the way, Modena and other cities in the region were not far behind. In fact, as we discuss in more detail in the appendix, Malaguzzi worked with educators and families to establish the first *scuole dell'infanzia* in Modena in the early 1960s.

Over time *scuole dell'infanzia* developed in Reggio Emilia and Modena in separate, but very similar ways in terms of the structure, organization, and curricula of the schools. We consider now some of the basic similarities and differences in the present-day schools that we can document based on the many publications regarding the Reggio Emilia approach and our own experiences through several years of observations in Giuseppe Verdi preschool in Modena.

In terms of general administrative structure, the *scuole dell'infanzia* in Reggio Emilia and Modena are very similar. There are several coordinators who are in charge of working with teachers and families of the schools in the city. Their position is termed *pedagogista*. Also the general structure of individual schools is very much alike with children normally in three age groups of 3-, 4-, and 5-year-olds with two teachers for each group. The children in both cities normally stay together with the same teachers for all 3 years of preschool.

Despite the structural similarities of the *scuole dell'infanzia* in the two cities, there are some organizational differences in staffing and programs. The Reggio Emilia program is noted for the *atelier* that exists in all its schools. The *atelier* is a special space in the school that could best be described in English as a studio or laboratory. It is a place of provocation, creativity, and production (Gandini, Hill, Cadwell, & Schwall, 2005; Malaguzzi, 1998). The activities in the *atelier* are organized by an *altelierista* who has a special function working alongside of or separate from the teachers. Although much of the activity in the *atelier* involves making art of various types, it is fair to say that the *altelierista* is not simply an art teacher. Vecchi (1998) argues that the *atelier* serves two functions in the schools in Reggio Emilia: "First, it provides a place for children to become masters of all kinds of techniques, such as painting, drawing, and working clay—all the symbolic languages. Second, it assists the adults in understanding processes of how children learn" (p. 140). By her second point, Vecchi means that the *atelier* helps teachers perceive and understand how children invent what she calls "autonomous vehicles of expressive freedom, cognitive freedom, symbolic freedom, and paths of communication" (p. 140). The *atelier* is also a space in which other activities in the school are preserved and documented for the children, teachers, parents, and anyone who visits the school.

Although the *atelier* exists in some preschools in Modena, it is not a general feature of the schools, and Giuseppe Verdi preschool did not have a distinct *atelier* or an *altelierista*. However, many of the artistic and other activities Vecchi describes were part of the curriculum inasmuch as the teachers constantly worked with the children on a variety of artistic projects, most of which were to reproduce and preserve short-term and long-term projects over the school year. Art creation was normally carried out in small groups with both teachers working with the children. The artistic projects, which included paintings, drawings, and clay sculptures, were displayed throughout the school. Also, as we will discuss in Chapter 3, when children in Modena took field trips to art museums, special teachers worked with the regular teachers in experiencing the museum's exhibitions and designed special art projects related to the exhibitions. Nonetheless, it is fair to say that the space and functions of the *atelier* were not as extensive in Modena as in Reggio Emilia, even if there did exist something similar.

Although most preschools in Modena do not contain an *atelier* and a specialized art teacher, they do have specialized instruction and staff for music and language. As we describe in the appendix, the children in each age group of the preschool have 2 hours per week of music with a specialized teacher, and the 4- and 5-year-olds also have English lessons (1 hour a week for 4-year-olds and 2 hours a week for 5-year-olds) conducted by native speakers of English. All of the children continued to study English after they made the transition to elementary school.

Perhaps Reggio Emilia is most known for the general philosophy and curriculum of its preschools. Cadwell (2003) has distilled what she terms are the fundamentals of the Reggio approach into a list of essential elements:

The child as protagonist
The child as collaborator
The child as communicator
The environment as third teacher
The teacher as partner, nurturer, and guide
The teacher as researcher
The documentation as communication
The parent as partner
The organization as foundational (p. 5)

Given the influence of Loris Malaguzzi and Bruno Ciari on early education in all of Emilia-Romagna, it is not surprising that this philosophy and curriculum has spread throughout the region and is clearly evident in schools in Modena as well as Reggio Emilia.

We discuss many of the features listed above in the appendix and in Part II, but here we stress just three of the points. The first is "teacher as researcher." In Modena, teachers experience only the beginning of their training before they enter the classroom. Much of their training and development takes place in the classroom, in special courses and seminars, and most especially in weekly meetings with all teachers and other staff in the individual schools. In meetings that we observed at Giuseppe Verdi there was always a great deal of lively debate, discussion, and expression of a variety of points of view. Rather than seen as potentially troubling, such debate was highly valued. Discussion and debate among the children were also a central part of morning meeting time in the school we studied.

The second point is "documentation as communicating," which Cadwell (2003) describes as follows:

> teachers' commentary on the purposes of the study and children's learning process, transcriptions of children's verbal language (i.e., words and dialogue), photographs of their activity, and representations of their thinking in many media are composed in carefully designed panels or books to present the process of learning in the schools. (p. 5)

In Giuseppe Verdi all these forms of documentation were a central part of the curriculum, especially in morning discussions, in the children's artistic productions, and in each child's protocol book that captured key events and activities of her or his life in the school and family during the 3 years in the preschool.

The third point, "parent as partner," refers to the importance of involvement of parents as well as extended family and the community in preschool education. At Giuseppe Verdi this involvement was evident in the parents and grandparents visiting with children, teachers, and each other in a leisurely way when they brought their children into the classroom each morning and picked them up in the afternoon. Participation was also evident in parent-teacher meetings throughout the year, at meetings of the parents organization (the *consiglio di gestione*), during special field trips planned by parents, at parties and festivities related to holidays, and especially at end of the year parties.

There is no doubt that Reggio Emilia early education is among the best in the world and deserves the great amount of attention that it has received. It is also true that Reggio casts a big shadow that tends to block out the high quality and progressive early education that exists in Modena, in other cities of the entire Emilia-Romagna region, and especially in the school we studied, Giuseppe Verdi.

THE RESEARCH CONTEXT

The particular methods of any study have both strengths and limitations. In this study we have relied on an ethnographic approach and a longitudinal design to document and understand transition processes in early childhood, most especially the transition from preschool to elementary school among a group of Italian children. Procedures of data collection such as units, types and sampling of field notes, and audiovisual data were similar to those we have employed and describe in detail elsewhere (Corsaro, 1985, 1994; Corsaro & Molinari, 2000a, 2000b). Here we summarize our database and discuss data analysis procedures. We also make clear the strengths and limits of a longitudinal case study of this type.

Rich Database

Earlier we noted that Bill was accepted by the teachers and children and over time became an adult friend to the children. We do not claim that Bill was seen as a fellow peer by the children, but we do believe that he was accepted into their worlds and gained their perspectives in the preschool, their transition to first grade, and their progress throughout elementary school.

Overall, Bill collected detailed field notes based on hundreds of hours of participation observation in the preschool and elementary school. These materials are especially rich in detail and in the perspective of the children because Bill was on a fairly equal basis with the children in their lessons in the Italian language—he may have actually been less competent than several of the children. Bill did, of course, have more knowledge of mathematics in first through third grade; but by fourth grade the children's math assignments had become challenging to him, and he often struggled with some of the assignments, even asking the children for help. On the other hand, in preschool and in third through fifth grade Bill was seen as a competent adult in the children's instruction in English. But still he was seen not as a teacher, but as an adult friend who could offer help and encouragement.

Bill's integration into the peer culture in both the preschool and first grade put him in a position to enter into activities and conversations to which the teachers were not privy. The resulting observations were important in Bill's participation in interviews in which he mainly probed certain responses of children, parents, and teachers based on his knowledge of the school and peer cultures.

In addition to the observational data, we collected a detailed and rich set of interviews with a group of eight children and their parents as well as the teachers over a 6-year period beginning in preschool and continuing until the last year of elementary school. We also interviewed the group of eight children and their parents in their second year of middle school.

Luisa and Bill worked together in interviewing the teachers. Bill worked with a research assistant, Silvia Zetti, in the interviews of the eight children and their parents in preschool and elementary school, with Luisa participat-

ing in some of these interviews. For the interviews of the children and their
parents in middle school, Bill was able to work alone because his Italian had
improved considerably and he had come to develop strong personal relationships with his respondents.

We also collected a number of artifacts including children's artwork,
pictures of classroom displays, children's lessons from workbooks or teacher
handouts, and letters and gifts sent to Bill by the children.

Interpretive Analysis

Our general approach to data analysis is inductive and interpretive. First,
we constructed *thick descriptions* (Geertz, 1973) of the school and peer cultures as well as the children's lives outside the school to some degree. From
patterns in these descriptions we generated interpretive narratives that captured the meaning of these cultures in line with our theoretical approach of
interpretive reproduction (see Chapter 2) in comparison with earlier work on
children's peer cultures in preschools (Corsaro, 1985, 1992, 1994, 2003, 2005).

In addition, in this particular study we were interested in developing an
interpretive understanding of changes in children's lives (most especially the
transition from preschool to elementary school) and how the children's (as
well as their parents' and teachers') perceptions and social representations
of these changes were grounded in what we identified as *priming events* (see
Chapter 2 for further discussion).

An early pattern in our field notes was that the children, while they had
generated a rich peer culture in the preschool in terms of play routines, friendships, and collective participation in educational activities, were often prospecting to the coming transition to first grade. This prospecting to their futures
in elementary school could be seen in patterns in the data regarding their
concerns about more structured lessons, less time for free play, and their
increasing abilities in reading and writing. They often talked of what it would
be like in first grade, making references to experiences of siblings, relatives,
or friends. We also identified patterns in the school culture and curriculum
which were in line with our notion of priming events.

These patterns were developed further in our analysis of the first set of
interviews with the preschool children, parents, and teachers. In these interviews we found that the perceptions of parents and teachers of the coming
transition overlapped considerably with those of the children and were in
line with features of the curriculum that we earlier identified as important.
However, in our search for exceptions to clear patterns, or what we term
negative cases (see Rizzo, Corsaro, & Bates, 1992), we found that the children's perceptions and concerns about the transition differed in some ways
from those of their parents and teachers.

The power of longitudinal ethnography is that we were able to follow the children in their actual transition and to verify aspects of continuity and discontinuity and how these aspects were related to the priming events we identified. For example, we found that perspectives about the importance of siblings, relatives, or friends were actually played out in collective actions as these older children visited and supported the first graders in the first weeks of school in break times and during recess (discussed in more detail in Chapter 6). We were also able to see firsthand the nature of children's adjustment to more structured learning and their continued acquisition of literacy skills and how these adjustments and increasing skills were related to aspects of both the preschool and elementary school curriculum.

Finally, our intricate knowledge of the Italian preschool and elementary school system and its actual practice in Modena allowed us to pursue theoretical ideas regarding how macro features of the society, such as educational policies and school structure, enable and constrain children's peer culture and educational activities and achievement in preschool and elementary school. Comparisons with the educational policy and the structure of early education in the United States allowed us to develop policy implications that we grounded in clear points of articulation between macro factors, collective actions between teachers and students, and the children's collective agency in their peer cultures (Corsaro, Molinari, & Rosier, 2002).

Limitations

Because this is a case study, it cannot be generalized to all of Italy. We do not attempt to do so, and here our design is different from that of a larger study that might rely on less detailed observations of a much larger sample. Such designs allow for greater generalizability, but often at the sacrifice of detail and validity of observations, which characterize our study. Also, we do know that the schools we studied were typical of the city of Modena in size, general philosophy and curriculum, resources, and training and experience of teachers. As we have said, the Modena preschool system shares many of these same features with other preschools in the Emilia-Romagna region including the well-known preschools in Reggio Emilia. On the other hand, we know less about elementary schools throughout the region so we need to qualify our interpretations in the following chapters accordingly.

Finally, our aim was to focus on a specific group of children and their experiences in preschool and elementary school. Although our interviews allow us to document the preschool experiences, transition process, and adjustment and progression in elementary school for eight children in particular, we were not able to give the same attention to the other 70 children whom we observed in the course of the study. Some important questions were thus left unanswered and could be the basis of other studies. For example, we can speak only generally to the transition experiences of children with special needs or immigrant children who attended the preschool and elementary school. Our observations suggest that keeping children in the same group with the same teachers was especially beneficial for children with special needs, but it would take another study focusing on them specifically to develop such a finding more fully. Also, keeping children together and attendance in preschool was clearly helpful for the development of the language skills and enculturation of immigrant children. However, we can say little more than that as only one immigrant child was among the 16 children we followed from preschool to elementary school. Unfortunately, this particular child's parents did not agree to participate in the interview component of our study. Here again we feel research is needed and we hope the observations we did make can spur such research in the future.

Having made these qualifications, we feel we were successful in entering the worlds of the children we studied, in gaining their perspectives, and in documenting social, cultural, and educational processes crucial to their early education experiences. We also believe that our detailed interviews of the children, their parents, and teachers add to the depth and richness of our observational data.

A Framework for Understanding Children's Early Life Transitions

On a warm day in early May 1996, Bill Corsaro accompanied the children and teachers from the Giuseppe Verdi preschool on a visit to the elementary school most of them would attend in September. After the short walk to the school, the group stopped outside the school gate. One of the teachers, Carla, reminded the children to be on their best behavior. She told them that they would be visiting classrooms and laboratories and that they would meet their future first-grade teachers. Carla also pointed out that older, fifth-grade children would help guide them through the school and classrooms. The fifth graders were in their last year with the teachers who would be teaching the first graders next year.

All the children were excited and a bit nervous about the visit. They liked the idea of meeting their future teachers and getting attention from the older kids. As the group made its way through the entrance to the courtyard of the school, Carla again reminded the children not to run, to stay together, and to be quiet in the school hallways. Once the group was inside the courtyard, 15 fifth graders and two teachers who were standing near the entrance of the school began to clap and cheer. The elementary school teachers came down to greet the preschoolers, touching them on the face or patting them on the head. Then the preschoolers joined the fifth graders, and we all made our way into the school. So began what we call an important priming event and an important step in the preschoolers' transition to elementary school.

THE SIGNIFICANCE OF THE PRESCHOOL TO ELEMENTARY SCHOOL TRANSITION

Children's entry into elementary school is a critical transition in their lives. As Ladd and Price note, "Early school transitions, such as the transition from preschool to kindergarten, are particularly important because the attitudes and reputations that may be established at the outset of grade school may follow children through many years of formal schooling" (1987, p. 1169). However, until recently there has been very little theoretical or empirical work on children's transition to elementary school (see Alexander & Entwisle, 1988; Corsaro & Molinari, 2000b; Corsaro, Molinari, & Rosier, 2002; Entwisle & Alexander, 1999; Pianta & Cox, 1999b; Rimm-Kaufman & Pianta, 2000).

One consistent finding in both quantitative and qualitative studies of children's transitions to elementary school is that attending preschool has positive effects on children's transition to first grade in terms of social adjustment and academic performance (Barnett, 1996; Consortium of Longitudinal Studies, 1983; Entwisle & Alexander, 1999). Yet, the lack of public preschools in the United States means many of the most needy children do not attend preschool or attend poor-quality private child care programs that offer little beyond custodial care. Furthermore, the comparative work that does exist shows that children's experiences and preparation in high-quality, government-supported preschools in Western Europe and in Japan put them at a strong advantage over American preschool children for making the transition to elementary school (see Corsaro, Molinari, & Rosier, 2002; for discussions of preschool programs in a range of modern societies, see Bergmann, 1996; Edwards, Gandini, & Forman, 1998; Lamb, Sternberg, Hwang, & Broberg, 1992; Tobin, Wu, & Davidson, 1991).

This book makes three important contributions to previous work on children's transitions to elementary school. First, it presents an interpretive theoretical perspective that conceptualizes transitions as collective processes that occur within social or institutional contexts. Second, it involves a methodology (comparative, longitudinal ethnography) that directly observes Italian children's transition from preschool to elementary school as we joined a group of children in their last year of preschool and made the transition with them to elementary school and then to middle school. With this method we fully explore, and to some degree participate in, the rich and complex history and development of the Italian early education system. We are also the first to investigate how children's experiences in this preschool system affect their transition to and progress in an Italian elementary school. Finally, the book examines the nature of social policy and practice in the Italian preschool and elementary school system and draws out the policy implications for better supporting children's transition to formal schooling in the United States.

We now turn to a discussion of our theoretical perspective and compare and contrast it with other theories of human development and socialization.

AN INTERPRETIVE APPROACH TO CHILDREN'S
TRANSITION TO ELEMENTARY SCHOOL

There are a wide variety of theoretical approaches to human development and socialization in psychology and sociology. Traditional theories of
socialization tend to view development as primarily the individual child's
internalization of adult skills and knowledge, and therefore focus on individual outcomes. Some of these theories paid more attention to children's
activity and agency than others. For example, the important work of con-
structivist theorists in psychology like Piaget (1950) and Vygotsky (1978)
were a valuable improvement over highly deterministic and behavioristic
theories in sociology and psychology, which primarily viewed children in a
passive role, molded by adult reinforcement or imitation of adult models
(Parsons & Bales, 1955).

More recent theoretical models in developmental psychology build on
and expand the insights of Piaget and Vygotsky. For example, children's
agency and the importance of social and cultural context is central to the
narrative approach of Bruner (1986), systems theories (Thelen & Smith,
1998), sociocultural theory (Rogoff, 2003), and new conceptualizations of
Piagetian theory (Tesson & Youniss, 1995). These theories call for a movement away from searching for underlying competencies or causes for human
development and stress the importance of direct studies of developmental
processes over time and space.

Interpretive Reproduction

Using a series of comparative ethnographies of peer interaction and culture over the last 30 years, we have developed a theoretical approach to
childhood socialization that we call *interpretive reproduction*, which is generally in line with these trends in approaches to human development in psychology (Corsaro 1992, 1993, 2005; Corsaro & Miller, 1992; for other
examples of the interpretive approach to childhood socialization, see James,
Jenks & Prout, 1998; Mayall, 2002; Thorne, 1993). The term *interpretive*
captures innovative and creative aspects of children's participation in society. Children produce and participate in their own unique peer cultures by
creatively appropriating information from the adult world to address their
own concerns. The term *reproduction* captures the idea that children are not
simply internalizing society and culture, but are also contributing to cultural
production and change. The term also implies that children are, by their very
participation in society, constrained by the existing social structure and by
social reproduction.

Although many developmental psychologists have stressed the importance of children's agency and now recognize that social and cultural context is important, they often view context in static terms, as a variable affecting individual development. However, from the perspective of interpretive reproduction, cultural context is not a variable that affects development; rather, cultural context is a dynamic that is continually constituted in routine practices collectively produced at various levels of organization. Even when developmental psychologists visualize context as something that is collectively produced, primary concern usually remains with how these collective processes get inside the individual child and not the collective processes themselves.

An imaginative exercise may help to explain what we mean by interpretive reproduction. First, imagine that there is no such thing as individual development. Imagine that we develop as part of collective processes to which we contribute constantly in our interactions with others. Forget about internalization (or intrapersonal processes in Vygotsky's sense), but instead focus on the interpersonal and collective processes. Try to imagine these collective processes only. These collective processes are what we are interested in, and we want to document how these processes change over time in childhood.

Children do, of course, develop individually, but throughout this development the collective processes, which they are always part of, are also changing. These processes are most accurately viewed as occurring in the interwoven local or microcultures making up children's worlds (Geertz, 1983). When we discuss these collective processes developmentally or longitudinally, we must consider the nature of children's *membership* in these local cultures and the changes in their degree or intensity of membership and participation over time. We also must consider how different structural and institutional features constrain and enable the collective processes of interest. From this view, human development—or perhaps better phrased, the development of humans—is always collective, and transitions are always collectively produced and shared with significant others.

Priming Events

Crucial to the nature of membership is participation in collective routine activities that signify that one is part of a group and collective action. At the same time, cultural practices in these routines prepare, or prime, members for future transitions. Along these lines, we have developed the notion of *priming events* (Corsaro & Molinari, 2000b). Priming events involve activities in which children, by their very participation, attend prospectively to ongoing or anticipated changes in their lives. Such events are crucial to children's social construction of representations of temporal aspects of their lives (including important life transitions) because children's social representations do not arise from simply thinking about social life but rather from their collective, practical activities with others.

The concept of priming events shares certain features with a concept often referred to in sociology: Merton's *anticipatory socialization*. However, priming events, because they are part of identifiable collective actions, provide empirical grounding to Merton's more abstract concept.

Merton sees anticipatory socialization as a function of reference groups and defines it as "the acquisition of values and orientations found in statuses and groups in which one is not yet engaged but which one is likely to enter" (1968, p. 438). Although Merton notes that anticipatory socialization can occur through formal education and training, he argues that much of such preparation "is *implicit, unwitting*, and *informal*" (p. 439).

Anticipatory socialization is frequently cited in work on childhood and adult socialization. Yet there was no inductive empirical grounding of the concept in Merton's presentation nor has there been a tradition of empirical research on the concept in the area of childhood socialization. In Merton's discussion, children themselves are not mentioned, but we can infer that the socialization he implies, even if not didactic is still something that is completed with the appraisals of those with more power; in the case of children these appraisals come primarily from adult caretakers. Merton's contention that anticipatory socialization is unwitting and informal does imply some power or control to children and adults in the transitions in which they are participating, but determining the nature of this power or agency depends on investigation of empirical events. Such events and their characteristics are captured in the notion of priming events, which defines the processes more precisely as having interactive and communicative features that Merton only speculates about. Finally, as we will show in this study, priming events often involve the innovative productions of children within their peer cultures as well as input from adults.

INTERPRETIVE REPRODUCTION AND RECENT THEORIES OF HUMAN DEVELOPMENT AND LIFE TRANSITIONS

Although we have so far contrasted our notion of interpretive reproduction with traditional views of human development, our theoretical position is part of a broader questioning of individualistic approaches to human development referred to above. We have already mentioned the important contributions of Bruner (1986). System-based and ecological theories of human development and life transitions have also raised provocative questions about the limits of individual internalization of knowledge and skills for human development and life transitions (Bronfenbrenner & Morris, 1998; Rimm-Kauffman & Pianta, 2000; Thelen & Smith, 1998). In addition, work on the life course (Elder, 1974; 1994; Entwisle & Alexander, 1999) stresses the importance of social structure and development and how children's early life transitions "place them on various pathways that take them to their adult social positions" (Entwisle & Alexander, 1999, p. 14).

Most important for our work has been the refinement and extension of the theoretical views of Vygotsky in sociocultural theory (Lave & Wenger, 1991; Rogoff, 2003; Wertsch, 1998). We now turn to a consideration of each of these theoretical traditions and their relation to interpretive reproduction.

Sociocultual Theory

Our extension of the notion of interpretive reproduction to study children's life transitions strikingly parallels the theoretical and empirical work on this same topic by Rogoff (Rogoff, 1995, 1996). Rogoff argues that "questions about transitions can fruitfully be examined from a sociocultural perspective that asks how children's involvements in the activities of their community change, rather than focusing on change as a property of isolated individuals" (1996, p. 273). From this view, changes—including life transitions—"are neither exclusively in the individuals nor exclusively in their environments, but a characteristic of individuals' involvements in ongoing activity" (p. 273).

Rogoff stresses, as do we, the importance of children's changing participation in sociocultural activities and suggests they be studied on three different planes of analysis: the community, the interpersonal, and the individual. However, in line with our notion of interwoven local cultures, Rogoff notes that community, interpersonal, and individual processes cannot be analyzed as separate planes of analysis, but rather that all must be studied together with shifting foci (from background to foreground) through a community, interpersonal, or individual analytic lens (1996, pp. 280–281). Finally, Rogoff's notion of *participatory appropriation* fits nicely with our notion of priming events in that she argues that "any event in the present is an extension of previous events and is directed toward goals that have not yet been accomplished" (1995, p. 155). Thus previous experiences in collectively produced and shared activities are not merely stored in memory and called up in the present; rather "the person's previous participation contributes to the event at hand by having prepared it" (p. 155). In their research, Rogoff and her colleagues have applied this sociocultural approach to children's development through several studies (Mosier & Rogoff, 1995; Rogoff, 1995, 1996, 2003).

Despite the similarity of our theoretical position to that of sociocultural approaches and especially the work of Rogoff, there are some key differences. Our work has developed out of sociology and social psychology and stresses the importance of not only children's active and creative participation in society as a basis for the development of self and the appropriation of cultural values (Mead, 1934) but also the constraining nature of society and processes of social reproduction (see Bourdieu, 1977; Corsaro, 1993; Corsaro, Molinari, & Rosier, 2002; Giddens, 1991).

It is the latter focus (especially in regard to power relations connected with social-class position, race, ethnicity, and gender) that is often neglected in sociocultural approaches. When focusing on the macroplane of analysis, Rogoff and other sociocultural theorists are primarily concerned with variations in cultural values and their relation to various cultural practices. Like Rogoff we believe that cultural practices and values reinforce one another and contribute to cultural reproduction. However, aspects of social structure (most especially socioeconomic and power relations) affect how variations in values within a given culture constrain some social practices and empower others.

When comparing quite divergent cultures in regard to values and practices—such as modern Western societies, especially the middle and upper classes of the United States, with developing societies—variations in values and practices have clear implications for human development. Such comparisons, however, often fail to capture variations in values and practices within cultures that are related to power relations. Further, we argue that comparisons within and across Western societies not only capture the effects of power relations on values and practices, but also reveal how social policies established by political and cultural elites affect which practices and values are legitimized and which are seen as different or even deficient. In short, power relations and social inequalities are always central factors in the formation and legitimation of cultural values, cultural practices, and human development.

In this book we examine Italian children's collective actions and experiences in the family and school during their transition from preschool to elementary school. As in Rogoff's work, the community, interpersonal, and individual planes are preserved in the analysis. In addition, we focus on the children's interpersonal or collective actions with each other as being part of autonomous peer cultures that exist both alongside of and interwoven with the more general adult culture. Further, on the community plane we stress the importance of power relations and resulting social policies in Italy (related to early socialization, child care, and early childhood education) that affect and are affected by cultural values and that support or constrain children's transition to formal schooling.

Ecological Theories of Children's Transitions

Much of the theoretical and empirical work on children's transition to formal schooling (from the home or preschool to elementary school) has been done in the United States and focuses on the transition to kindergarten (Pianta & Cox, 1999b; Rimm-Kaufman & Pianta, 2000). Although some of this work includes minority children, children from economically disadvantaged groups, and children with special needs, a lack of comparative perspective (either across subcultural groups or societies) works against the consideration of the importance of power relations on policy formation that affects children's transitions.

However, the growing recognition of the importance of context and processual aspects of transitions is important. For example, Rimm-Kaufman & Pianta (2000) present an ecological and dynamic model of transition. This model differs from the more traditional child effects model, which focuses on how individual characteristics of children (poverty status, language abilities, ethnicity, temperament, and so on) affect their school adjustment. The child effects model is an input-output model that predicts that certain characteristics of children will affect transition outcomes but actual transitions are inferred or neglected.

Ecological models are sometimes offered as alternatives to the child effects model. These models focus on direct effects of context seen as static variables, such as characteristics of preschools and schools, family processes, and neighborhoods, as well as indirect effects, again seen as variables such as peer relations and family communication. However, these contextual models still lack any direct consideration of the actual collective processes that constitute transitions. Nor do these ecological models account for power relations and social policies, which produce and reproduce the very social contexts and networks they identify.

Rimm-Kaufman and Pianta offer a dynamic effects model influenced by systems theory (Pianta & Walsh, 1996) and the bioecological model of Bronfenbrenner and Morris (1998):

> [The dynamic effects model] posits that the transition to school takes place in an environment defined by the many changing interactions among child, school, classroom, family, and community factors. Child characteristics and contexts interact through a transactional process. These interactions, over time, form patterns and relationships that can be described not only as influences on children's development, but also as outcomes in their own right. (Rimm-Kaufman & Pianta, 2000, p. 499)

This recognition that children's worlds change as children develop is important, and for this reason Rimm-Kaufman and Pianta's call for longitudinal studies over the whole course of transitions is commendable. However, the dynamic effects model still falls short because of its assumption that human development (here the transition to formal schooling) is an individual process that can be ultimately captured, explained, and tested by some complex variable analysis based on differing characteristics of individual children and arrangements and variations of contexts. As we argued earlier, the development of humans is always collective and transitions are always collectively produced and shared with significant others. Further, we see cultural contexts as collectively produced at the interpersonal, community, and societal level, and the nature of these productive-reproductive processes cannot be adequately captured through categorical or variable analysis regardless of the level of complexity. We believe instead that children's early life transitions can be best explained by relying on comparative case analyses (see Abbott, 1992; Flyvbjerg, 2004).

Life Course Theory

A major strength of life course research is its insistence on situating the developing individual in historical time and structural or cultural place. Elder defined the life course as a "multilevel phenomenon, ranging from structural pathways through social institutions and organizations to the social trajectories of individuals and their developmental pathways" (1994, p. 5). The notion of priming events, or collective activities that impel social actors to attend prospectively to ongoing and anticipated changes in their lives, clearly can aid in the conceptualization and empirical investigation of the form and meaning of transitions over the life course.

However, work to date on the life course has seldom addressed the life transitions of young children and instead has focused on adolescents and adults (see Elder, 1974; Furstenberg, Cook, Eccles, & Elder, 2000). Interpretive reproduction falls in line with what Elder terms the four themes of the life course paradigm: "the interplay of human lives and historical times, the timing of lives, linked or interdependent lives, and human agency in choice making" (1994, p. 5).

The most engaging work from a life course perspective on the life transitions of young children is that of Alexander and Entwisle and their colleagues (Alexander & Entwisle, 1988; Alexander, Entwisle & Horsey, 1997; Entwisle, 1995; Entwisle & Alexander, 1999; Entwisle, Alexander, & Olson, 1997). This work impressively ties American children's early elementary school social adjustment and academic achievement to their families' economic resources and what Entwisle and Alexander call *psychological capital*. Psychological capital, which they argue can be independent of its social or economic capital, "is the ability of parents to interact with their children in ways that prompt cognitive growth" (Entwisle & Alexander, 1999, p. 23). Obviously, collective interactions between parents and children that promote cognitive growth as well as particular social interactive styles that correspond with those of the majority middle-class school system can be seen as priming events. It is exactly these types of collective priming events in the home with adults and siblings and in the preschool and first grade with teachers and peers that we see as crucial for the nature of children's transitions (whether they be continuous or discontinuous) from preschool to elementary school (Corsaro, Molinari, & Rosier, 2002; Heath, 1983; Rosier, 2000).

In their work, Alexander, Entwisle, and their colleagues have not examined these priming events directly. They have, instead, identified the importance of such social and psychological capitals indirectly through the rigorous documentation in Baltimore schools of variations in children's academic performance in the early elementary school grades by race, social class, and over time.

Entwisle and Alexander also found that children of low socioeconomic status (SES) "were given lower marks, held back more often, and in other ways rated less favorably by teachers than were the high-SES children" (1999, p. 21). In short, the children were treated and graded differently despite making similar gains on standardized tests (even though they may have started out at lower levels). Thus, when we put the children's transition in historical and social context—the key focus of a life course perspective—we see different social pathways developing for poor compared to middle- and upper-class children. Again, however, as was the case in the family, in large-scale longitudinal studies like these we do not know precisely how interactions between teachers and students contribute to such differential treatment and transitional difficulties or discontinuities for the poor children. We know from intensive ethnographic studies that differences in priming events in preschool and the family, teacher perceptions of students, and miscommunications between teachers and students and teachers and parents can contribute to these variations in early school transitions and achievement by social class, race, and ethnicity (see Corsaro, Molinari & Rosier, 2002; Delpit, 1992; Heath, 1983; Rosier, 2000). It is these interactive patterns at the microlevel that we focus on in the case study making up this book.

However, Alexander and Entwisle's use of the life course approach in line with status attainment theory is of crucial importance for the aims of our case study. Their work captures how in the United States educational policy, socioeconomic structure, and power relations have dramatic constraining or enabling effects on children's transition to and progress in elementary school (in a large urban city like Baltimore). Their work will serve as a comparative base for our examination of some of these same macrofactors in Italy as we examine how Italian educational policy, power relations, and socioeconomic structure constrain or enable Italian children's transition from preschool to elementary school in Modena.

CONCLUSION

Overall, in this book our analysis is built on our theory of interpretive reproduction. However, in interpreting the data and drawing implications for further theoretical development and for educational policies, we build on and integrate our work with the existing theories and research we have reviewed in this chapter. In this way we add to the small (but growing) corpus of existing work on children's transition to elementary school, and we also can estimate the generalizability of our findings and discuss directions for future research.

PART II

Living, Learning, and Preparing for Change at Giuseppe Verdi Preschool

Building a Community of Learners and Looking to the Future: Priming Events in the School Culture

Bill had been a part of the group at Giuseppe Verdi preschool for about 6 weeks when he and the children gathered in the kitchen of the school to watch one of the teachers, Giovanna, demonstrate how to make Easter cake. She poured out the flour on the big table, and then pushed it away with rounding motions of her hands to make a large hole in the center. She then cracked and dropped the eggs into the center, folded them into the flour, and kneaded the dough again and again. Finally, she broke off pieces of dough for everyone, to work with their own hands to prepare individual cakes for baking. As he kneaded his dough, Bill reflected on the previous 6 weeks and how he, like the eggs, had been folded, enveloped, and kneaded into the peer and school cultures of this group. Although not yet a full member of the group, Bill's experience helps to capture the overall nature of the strong social integration in this group of children and their teachers.

In this chapter we examine the nature of social relations in the school culture at Giuseppe Verdi. (Peer culture is explored in Chapter 4). First we describe the school routines and then turn to a focus on priming events for the coming transition to elementary school. Some of the priming events were formal in that their acknowledged purpose was to prepare children for the coming transition (e.g., two visits to the elementary school in May), but others were more subtle and deeply integrated into everyday activities in the preschool throughout Bill's 5 months of observations.

SCHOOL ROUTINES

We identified several types of routine activities in the school culture at Giuseppe Verdi. By *routine*, we mean that the collectively produced activities were recurrent and predictable. The repeated production of such routines is important because it provides children and all other social actors with the security and shared understanding of belonging to a social group (Bourdieu, 1977; Corsaro, 1992). On the other hand, the predictability of routines provides numerous possibilities for creative embellishment in which social actors can interpret, produce, display, and extend a wide range of sociocultural knowledge. Since priming events in the preschool were often embedded in the production of routines in the school and peer cultures, projective social representations of the future, especially the coming transition to elementary school, emerged and were further cultivated in these everyday collective activities.

Morning Meeting Time

The central routine in the culture of the preschool was the morning meeting. These meetings were held every day after a morning snack, and normally lasted 45 minutes to an hour. The meetings usually began with general talk about plans for the day; on Mondays or after holidays there were detailed discussions about things the children had done and experienced in their days away from school. In every case, the first part of the meeting set the general tone of the overall meeting time itself, to give all the children an opportunity to have something to say or contribute as members of the group.

Sometimes discussion of plans for the day and personal experiences took up most, if not all, of the meeting time. The discussions were lively with all of the children participating and frequently interrupting each other to offer their opinions and thoughts on the comments of their teachers and peers. The Italian phrase, *secondo me* ("in my opinion") often preceded long turns at talk by a particular child with other children and the teachers quick to respond in agreement or disagreement. The importance placed on *discussione* of this type has been well documented in Italian schools and families (Corsaro, 2003, 2005; Corsaro & Rizzo, 1988; Orsolini & Pontecorvo, 1992; Pontecorvo, Fasulo, & Sterponi, 2001).

During meeting time there was also a strong display of emotion and community. The teachers were often physically affectionate with the children, but also joked and teased and were not hesitant to enter into disputes and debates with the children. Bill was especially taken with how natural the teachers and children were about physical affection. The teachers would often have children on their laps, give them hugs, kisses on the cheek, and playfully tussle their hair. Bill was also struck by the small amount of competition among the children for the teachers' attention (something that was common in the American middle-class preschools he studied). The teachers had different children on their laps at meeting time each day. Bill found the same thing happening to him as day to day one child and then another would hop up on his lap or grab him by the arm to pull him into play.

The teachers and children's interactive style during meeting time is undoubtedly related to the nature of presentation of self in Italian culture. But there is more to it than that. There had developed a strong sense of community and trust in this group, which had been together on an everyday basis for nearly 3 years—a key element in the Italian early education philosophy (Corsaro & Emiliani, 1992; Malaguzzi, 1998).

Often after general discussion about plans for the day or happenings over weekends or vacation, the morning meeting time involved reflections on and re-creations of short- and long-term projects. One such project (a short project that lasted a few weeks) involved discussions and children's drawings related to the human body. In one morning meeting in the last month of the school year the teacher, Carla, introduced a discussion of the project.

The children are seated in red chairs in a semicircle with Carla in the center. One part of the semicircle is in front of walls decorated with artwork related to school projects and the other side is in front of a large glass window through which abundant sunshine lights up the room. Maria, the substitute teacher for Giovanna (who is on family leave), sits at the edge of the semicircle on the left. Bill is videotaping the discussion. Carla has the children's drawings on her lap, and she will eventually discuss each child's drawing with the group. The children are excited because they have enjoyed this project and producing their drawings, and now they will each have the opportunity to talk about their work. Before commenting on the individual drawings, Carla initiates some general discussion about the project.

"Is there a way to discover or understand if there is something inside our body?" Carla asks.

"To do x-rays," says Marina.

"To do x-rays?" asks Carla "What is it useful for? What can you see with them?"

"To see if there is something inside," replies Sonia.

"And what?" asks Carla.

Several children shout out, "The bones!"

"With x-rays you can see the bones and what else?" asks Carla.

Sofia now responds, "The brains, the lungs."

"The heart!" shouts Carlotta.

"The heart and then other things," says Carla.

Several children now say, "The lung, the heart."

"The lung, the heart, we already said these. And what else?" asks Carla.

"The blood," Elisa responds.

"The arteries," says Marina.

"How can you see the blood?" asks Maria (the substitute teacher).

Several children are talking at once, "When we cut ourselves, when we get hurt or injured."

"Yes," replies Carla, "with x-rays we can see what is inside our body. All of the things we have inside our body that we cannot see because our body is not transparent. But if you touch yourself you can imagine something."

Several children say, "Yes, the bones."

Other children say, "The veins."

There is a lot of talk and commotion now, but Carla stays calm. Sofia and Sandra leave their seats and walk up to Carla holding out their arms to show their veins. The other children who remain seated hold out their arms to each other to inspect their veins that are visible beneath their skin.

Sofia now returns to her seat and Carla says, "We can see the veins because our skin is a little transparent."

Luciano now gets up and walks over to Carla and says, "Look," as he holds out his arm.

Sandra now starts back to her seat and then stops and makes a muscle with her arm and holds her other hand on the muscle getting Carla's attention.

"Oh, that's true," says Carla. "We can feel the muscles!" She makes a muscle like Sandra and all the other children do so as well. There is a lot of talking about feeling their muscles.

"I know a game," says Viviana. "It is a game of . . ." She stops to think of the name of the game.

"Popeye!" shout several children.

"But what are you saying!" responds Viviana, denying that Popeye is the game she has in mind.

Viviana is sitting right next to Carla, who pats Viviana's leg and says, "Now you take your time to think about it. And then you will tell us."

"And we can also hear some noises inside our body that help us to understand," says Carla.

"The belly!" shouts Luciano.

"When the belly growls," say several children.

"Sometimes we can hear some noises," says Carla.

Several children now shout out and it is difficult to understand them.

"One at a time," says Maria.

"What kind of noises are coming from our stomach?" asks Carla.

"When it growls," says Carlotta.

"Growls when?" asks Carla.

"When we are hungry," answers Sofia.

Throughout this discussion the teacher, Carla, has asked a number of questions and built on the children's answers. The discussion is often animated with several children talking at once and others leaving their seats to make their points and get individual attention. While someone who had not visited this class before may think things are a bit out of control at times, Carla is very patient and gives children the opportunity to express their knowledge and opinions. We see that the children become even more involved as Carla continues to ask questions.

"When we are hungry, we can hear the stomach growling," says Carla. "From this we understand that we have a stomach. And then what else?"

"If we put our hand here," says Marina as she touches her chest, "we can feel the heart. And also [now Marina touches her wrist] the pulse."

"How can you hear the heart? What do you feel?" asks Carla.

"The heartbeat. Like this," says Marina as she pats her chest and makes thumping sounds. "And if you put that instrument in your ears like this," Marina now takes the headband from her head and places it in her ears, "and there is that other part and you put it here," says Marina as she touches her chest. "It is a way to hear it better."

"Like the doctor does," says Renato.

"My grandfather has one of these," says Marina.

"What is the name of that instrument? Do you know?" asks Carla.

"I don't know," says Marina.

"Stethoscope," says Carla.

Marina replies, "My grandfather is not a doctor, he is . . ."

"Are there other things that you understand you have inside—you understand them because you hear some noises?" says Carla.

"The veins," offers Sonia.

"The veins because you see them," says Carla. "We said so. What else?"

"The eyes because we see them in the mirror," says Stefania.

"The tonsils," says Viviana.

"The tonsils?" repeats Carla. "How do you know that you have them?"

"Because I had tonsillitis," says Viviana.

"Ah, that's true" Carla agrees. "You know it because sometimes some part of your body gets ill."

Sandra points to her throat and says, "I had tonsillitis. My throat was red."

"So there are things we have that we don't feel, but then they are hurt and so one understands that they exist. For example, when your tonsils are inflamed and the doctor says, 'You have tonsillitis.' So you understand here in your neck [Carla touches her neck] because he looks into your throat. Then, for example, what were you operated for recently?" Carla asks Sonia.

"Appendicitis," Sonia responds.

"What is appendicitis? Did you see it?" asks Carla.

"No," says Sonia shyly.

"But you were feeling it, weren't you?" asks Carla.

"A piece of the guts that has been inflamed," says Luciano.

"Luca says that the appendix is a piece of the guts," the substitute teacher Maria says approvingly.

"In my opinion it is a gut that is rotten," adds Elisa.

Now there is a lot of excitement as Luciano and Irene try to say something but cannot be heard because several other children are talking.

"Let Irene talk," says Maria.

"It is a bag that goes in the part of the body and makes appendixes," notes Irene.

"Do you know that my aunt has never been operated on for appendicitis when she was a child," adds Sonia.

"Neither was I," says Carla. "It is like the tonsils, sometimes they are healthy."

"It is because you eat too much chocolate," claims Sofia.

"Not only that," says Carla.

Viviana now remembers the game she could not think of earlier and says, "Carla, now I thought of the name of the game. Its name is the game of the human body. You can see the muscles, the heart, the tonsils."

Sonia adds, "When you go to school, you study the human body."

At this point Carla holds up the papers on her lap and draws the children's attention to them.

"Now when we gave you this piece of paper there was only the outline of the human body, and we asked you to draw what you thought was inside the body," says Carla. "The things that we cannot see, but we can think are there because if we touch we can feel the bones, the muscles, and the heart beating, and we can hear the stomach growling. Each one of you drew what you imagined was inside the body. Who wants to come and show us?"

Several children shout, "Me! Me!"

"We start with Marina," says Carla. And Marina comes up to Carla and takes her picture.

This example of meeting time talk near the end of the school year shows the strong sense of community and participation of the children. It also shows a skilled teacher who wants to go beyond a review and reproduction of the children's work on a project, to engage the children in an "intellectual dialogue" in which she joins the children in creating "excitement and curiosity" (Edwards, 1998, p. 181). Carla does this by constantly asking questions, listening to the children's responses, and asking new questions. She skillfully develops most of the interesting topics raised by the children as they think again and in new ways about the human body:

- Sandra adds the touching of muscles to the seeing of veins.
- Viviana tries to think of the game related to the human body (which, when it comes to her much later, is ironically called the human body).

- Marina introduces the idea of hearing the heartbeat by way of a special instrument (the stethoscope), which she cleverly illustrates using her headband.
- Stefania notes you can see your eyes in the mirror.
- Viviana aptly introduces her experience with tonsillitis, which leads to the discussion of Sonia's recent experience of appendicitis.
- Luciano and Irene creatively describe the appendix and its place inside the body.
- Finally Sofia warns that too much chocolate can cause problems for the tonsils.

In descriptions of preprimary education in Reggio Emilia the metaphor of "catching the ball that the children throw us" is often mentioned (Edwards, 1998, p. 181). Carla provokes the throwing of a lot of balls by the children and she catches most of them (I would have liked for Carla to have responded "to seeing our eyes in the mirror") and throws them right back to the children. And the exciting dialogue, sometimes too exciting and leading to gentle calming, continues. And this is just a prelude to the reproduction through discussion of the children's individual work, which was still to come.

Long-Term Projects

In line with the general collectivist educational philosophy of Italian preschools (especially in the Emilia-Romagna region), there was a strong emphasis on documentation of shared collective activities both through language and discussion (as we just saw) and through artistic productions (Edwards et al., 1998). These verbal and artistic reproductions were central to another goal and an associated set of routines in Giuseppe Verdi: long-term projects.

Each year in the preschool, the teachers and children would jointly discuss and decide on two or three long-term projects that would involve a number of interrelated activities. For example, in the year of our study the teachers and children participated in a number of activities that were all related to the concept of light and dark. Some activities examined the actual physical nature of light and dark. For example, one day when the children and Bill returned from lunch, they entered the room to find themselves "completely in the dark," as the teachers, Carla and Giovanna, had turned off all the lights and covered all the windows. Carla took the hand of one child and asked that everyone hold hands. Eventually, following Carla's lead, everyone was seated on the floor. Carla and Giovanna said they could see better because their eyes had become accustomed to the dark, and after a few minutes the children and Bill would also be able to see better. The teachers waited a bit, and there was a lot of laughter and whispering in the dark. Then Carla moved an object covered by a cloth to the front of the group. Slowly removing the cloth, she asked the children to guess what it was. A few children complained that "they could not see it well enough," but then one child guessed correctly that it was the coat rack that usually sat in the corner of the room. The activity was repeated with several other objects, which were quickly identified as the children's eyes became accustomed to the dark. Then the teachers began little by little to remove the covers from the windows. They asked the children to describe the nature of the light and how it affected their eyes and ability to see things in the room. Finally, the teachers quickly removed the rest of the covering and turned on the lights in the room. Several of the children yelled, "Now it's too light!" and covered their eyes. The teachers explained that once our eyes become used to the dark, bright light is blinding, and our eyes must readjust. Finally, this presentation was followed by a discussion about nocturnal animals who sleep during the day and hunt for food in the dark because of the physical nature of their eyes.

Other activities related to light and dark during meeting time involved reading and discussing poems that described landscapes and the nature of light at sunrise, midday, early evening, and sunset. Several of these poems were quite abstract for 5-year-olds, but the children displayed a keen interest and actively described the images that the poems conjured up or reminded them of in their lives.

Later the children created numerous paintings and other artistic projects related to light and dark. In one activity, they cut out depictions of sunrises and sunsets from magazines. These pictures were then placed in the center of a white sheet of art paper, and the children, with help from the teachers, painted around the pictures so that they blended into an almost seamless painting. Bill marveled at the children's ability to mix paint to create the colors and hues in their paintings and the high quality of the children's productions, which were far beyond his own artistic abilities. These paintings were displayed on the walls of the school along with texts of poems and the children's responses to the poems to reconstruct aspects of the overall project.

The children's artistic productions served to intensify their involvement in a community of learning through their own personal contributions. The artwork was also prominently displayed, which not only reinforced the school culture, but documented the group's work together for parents and grandparents and others who visited the classroom on a regular basis.

Field Trips

Another central routine in the school culture was the *gita*, or field trip. A key aspect of the curriculum was to involve children in the daily life and culture of their city. During the 5 months Bill observed in the preschool, the numerous *gite* included visits to Modena's planetarium (which built on the project of light and dark), a botanical garden, a puppet show, a play, and an art museum. The visit to the art museum nicely captures the importance of field trips, not only for this particular class but for Modena's communal preschools more generally.

The teachers, children, and Bill boarded a bus that took them to a small park near the center of the city where the museum was located. It was a warm spring day and the children were allowed to explore the park, which contained a duck pond and some playground equipment. After about 30 minutes the teachers called for the children to go into the museum. The group was met by a woman who, Bill was later told, was an art teacher for all the preschools in the Modena commune. The first thing visible in the center of the museum was a collection of objects: pieces of wood and rubber, empty bottles and cans, small cardboard boxes, and other such things. Bill soon learned that the artist whose work was on display in the museum made sculptures from everyday objects that were often discarded as trash or recyclable material.

As Bill continued to inspect the large collection of objects, which were surely there for the children to make art productions of their own, the art teacher ushered everyone into one long corridor to the left where there were many displays of the artist's work. The children were seated in front of one production that looked something like the head of a bull (this was modern art and the images were abstract). The art teacher asked the children what they thought of the sculpture. Luciano immediately spoke up and gave a detailed 5-minute description of the sculpture and what he thought it signified. Bill thought Luciano saw a lot more in the art than he did. Other children also spoke up supporting or disagreeing with Luciano's evaluation. Thus the tour began and continued for a stop at each exhibit in the long corridor— at least 15 sculptures all in the modern and abstract style.

Bill was relieved when the group returned to the center of the museum. To his surprise, however, instead of staying there and making things with the provided materials, the group was escorted to the right corridor where another set of sculptures were displayed. Bill was already getting pretty bored and was amazed at how patient and interested the children remained. Each piece in this area of the museum was also examined and discussed, with the art teacher showing a good deal of pleasure in the children's enthusiastic responses.

Finally, the group returned to the center of the museum, and the children in groups of two and three made their own sculptures. The art teacher, Carla, and Giovanna all helped and gave advice, but the children mainly worked on their own. They produced many sculptures in the style of the artist.

Then it was time to go. The children's productions were to remain in the museum and be put on display in the center section. Bill was surprised that none of the children complained about leaving the work behind and asked Giovanna about it. She said that the children's work would be returned to the school when this particular exhibition ended in about 6 weeks.

At meeting time the next day the children discussed the visit to the museum. There was much talk about how the artist made good use of objects and materials that had been thrown in the trash. This led to a general discussion of the environment and the importance of recycling. After the meeting the children drew pictures that re-created the visit to the museum. Some drew the group on the bus, in the garden, or outside of the museum, while others drew images of the artist's work. These pictures were grouped on one wall of the school with text about the visit and the children's impressions of the art, which the teachers had recorded during the tour. Again we see the importance of production and reproduction through discussion and artwork in the school's curriculum. Here we also see how the group goes outside the school to participate in a cultural institution and preserves the experience in the reproductions.

Special Events

The children's involvement in the community through field trips was complemented by other special events in the school and the community. These events are noteworthy for the participation of parents and other family members and, in some cases, the wider community. For example, there was a party at the end of the year for the whole preschool and a special party just for the group we studied, organized by the parents and teachers. At these parties the kids performed dancing and singing routines they had practiced for many weeks. The parents and some grandparents also engaged in some of the dances and participated in games with the kids as well as providing pizza and other snacks. The parents gave the teachers expensive gifts (gold watches) and even provided a gift (a beautiful beach towel) for Bill as a member of the group.

Because our study followed the preschool children to first grade and we continued to observe the four first-grade classes throughout the 5 years of elementary school, we were able to observe and experience many of the events and activities in Modena in which a strong civic society was constructed around these children and their families. By civic society we mean a collective celebration of civic engagement, people's connections with and participation in the life of their communities (Putnam, 1993). In the United States, examples of such civic society might be neighborhood block parties, bowling leagues, union picnics, and ethnic street festivals. Although such events still exist, many argue that they are fading from the lives of Americans and their children (Putnam, 1996).

Civic engagement was strong in Modena and often involved, and even centered on, children. In fact, preschools and elementary schools were sometimes sites and kids the focus of many civic activities. In Chapter 1 we described one such event, the celebration of Carnevale in the preschool and city center. This was one of several special events that occurred both at the school and at the community level. Another was a concert of traditional children's songs performed by 5-year-olds from all the preschools for all the people of the city. This performance was preceded by months of preparation and practice by the children under the direction of the music teachers in each preschool. The concert, which occurred in mid-May, was a spectacular and highly successful civic event with many proud parents and grandparents in the large audience (Corsaro, 2003).

The children also gave a performance of the songs at another civic event in the preschool, the *festa dei nonni* ("party for grandparents"). Nearly all the grandparents of the kids who lived in Modena attended the *festa dei nonni*. The kids and grandparents worked together on many projects. Some grandmothers, with girls and boys, sewed clothes for dolls, while other grandmothers made desserts from traditional recipes with their grandchildren to have after lunch. One grandfather planted a garden in the outside yard with one group of kids, while another grandfather made kites. Later, the kids flew their kites in the outside yard with Bill given the job of retrieving wayward kites from the trees. Overall, it was a fun and memorable day for the grandparents, the kids, and the teachers (see Corsaro, 2003).

PRIMING EVENTS

The teachers and children at Giuseppe Verdi displayed a general awareness throughout the last months of the school term that the children would be expected to learn to read and write in first grade. This awareness was most apparent when certain of the children were encouraged and praised for their efforts to read sentences, phrases, and even short stories and for attempting to print their names and various words and phrases. Although not all of the children could or even tried to read and write, all were involved in projects in the curriculum that developed a positive orientation to literacy.

Literacy Projects

One general strategy was to encourage reading and writing as part of art projects. As we discussed previously, the children loved to draw and paint pictures and construct other types of artwork like collages, murals, and sculpture. One such project involved the combination of creating art and recognizing the first letters of their names. Here we summarize from field notes.

> After one teacher, Carla, read and discussed a story about a baby walrus with the children, the other teacher, Giovanna, comes and joins the circle and displays, one by one, pictures the children have produced for a particular project based on an earlier story read and discussed in the group. The project involves the children's drawing a picture with the first letter of their names framing or orienting the scene. For example, Mario drew a picture of mountains with the two peaks in "M" representing mountain peaks. Sandra drew a very impressive (both beautiful and imposing) snake in a jungle with the "S" of her name.
>
> Luciano's picture [see Figure 3.1] was very inventive in that he inverted the "L" of his first name to make it into a shower on a beach in Italy where he visited. His picture was embellished by many other things one finds at Italian beach resorts.

In one long-term project the teachers and the children carried out a number of literacy activities that involved reading, discussing, and reproduc-

Figure 3.1. Luciano's Drawing, Featuring His First Initial.

ing the story of the *Wizard of Oz*. The literacy activities occurred over a period of 5 months and involved several overlapping phases and types of activities.

In the first phase the teachers and children read the book over a period of about 4 months. They read a chapter or so a week usually in daily meetings that lasted about an hour. However, the teachers did not simply read the story and show pictures to the children. Rather each chapter was read, discussed, and debated. These debates were very lively, and children were encouraged to ask questions and to make comments. Nearly all of the children participated in each discussion, and in some meetings the children and teachers spent more time debating than actually reading.

In the second phase, during the reading of the last two chapters of the book, the teachers and children began work on a large mural depicting the Emerald Castle in the background and images of each of the four main characters—Dorothy, the Tin Man, the Lion, and the Scarecrow—standing in front of the castle. The children worked in small groups with the teachers designing various aspects of the highly complex and impressive artistic production. Group work on the art project lasted around 3 weeks.

In the third phase the teachers worked with the children one at a time. In these dyadic sessions the teachers asked children questions about the story, their favorite character, their favorite scene, and so on. The children's responses were recorded on audiotape. After the teacher printed out these responses for the children, the children copied their narratives into a small workbook. In this same workbook the children drew a picture of their favorite character and printed the name of the character under the picture. The teachers also pointed out to the children that they would be reading and writing on their own in first grade. These teacher-child sessions occurred over about a 3-week period.

In the fourth phase the children and teachers again discussed the story in a group meeting, and each child was asked to pick a different scene to re-create with a personal drawing. In the group discussion a set of scenes reproducing the entire story was decided upon, as well as which child would draw which scene. Over a 2–3-week period the children, working in small groups with the teachers, made sketches of their selected scenes. Each child then described his or her sketched scene to the teacher, and with spelling help printed out this description on a separate piece of paper. During these activities the teachers pointed out to the children that they would be writing on their own in this way in first grade.

Figure 3.2 shows Federica's sketch. She has drawn an air balloon floating in the clouds with two people on it. She printed her own description of the scene, which can be summarized into English (using her punctuation and grammar) as follows: "The wizard of oz and Dorothy went with an air

Figure 3.2. Federica's Sketch.

balloon to Dorothy's house because Dorothy wished to return home with her aunt and uncle to be happy." She then printed her name under the text.

Then the children, again working in small groups with the teachers, produced their sketches in paintings and collages. These productions were displayed on the classroom wall with the sketches beside each artistic production of the scenes. The children, teachers, and parents all observed and admired the productions.

In the fifth and final phase, during a meeting in the last week of school in late June, the teachers had the children take down their paintings. They then collectively reproduced the story a final time by having each child place his or her scene in the proper order on the floor in the middle of the discussion circle. Again as in the reading of the story, this exercise was done with a great deal of debate. On the last day of school the children took home their individual paintings as well as a book of photocopies of all the children's sketches and descriptions of the various scenes. Now they had their own copy of the *Wizard of Oz* that they had collectively produced.

In this group project lasting around 5 months, the children and the teachers participate in collective and individual activities that involve several literacy skills: reading, writing, understanding the structure and sequence of events in a story, and depicting and reproducing the story artistically. Thus the children with the help of their teachers reconstruct and appropriate a literacy event in an individual and collective way.

Overall, the projects introduce the children to new knowledge and encourage their development of social, cognitive, and literacy skills. In addition, the teachers at various points in the projects called the children's attention to the fact that they would perform similar literacy tasks in first grade. Further, since the projects occur over historical periods in which collective and individual contributions are made, discussed, evaluated, and reproduced, the children are impelled in a natural way to anticipate changes in their everyday activities in the school and in their lives more generally. As a result, the projects can be seen as preparing or priming children for elementary school where they will be participating in similar literacy activities and using and developing further their cultural knowledge and literacy skills.

Homework Assignments

Also during the last months of school the teachers began to focus more directly on literacy using homework assignments, or *i compiti*. In our first few months of observations, homework occasionally was assigned on weekends. Usually the children discussed some aspects of ongoing projects with parents, and then carried out a related artistic activity. For example, during the project of light and dark the children were asked to watch a sunset or sunrise with their parents, discuss the experience, and draw a picture for class. In this way the children were introduced to the responsibility of completing weekend homework, which they were told would be assigned regularly in elementary school.

In another example that we recorded in field notes, the teachers extended the notion of weekend homework to individual performance in class by introducing the idea of "homework in class."

> Carla describes a work sheet and then hands it out to the children, but has them work separately on individual seats which are turned over to serve as desks rather than work at tables as a group. She refers to this as *i compiti in classe*—"homework in class." The children kneel in front of the seats to work and tell others not to copy from them. Later, this becomes somewhat disruptive as children move extra chairs to block others and keep them farther away. For some kids, this blocking off of other children becomes more important than the actual work. The teachers see this activity, but ignore it.

Here, for the first time in preschool, the children were asked to do individual work separated from each other. The teacher's definition of the activity as "homework in class" identified it as an individual educational assignment of the type that would be typical in the first grade, where the children would sit at separate desks and do their own work. With their concern about copying, the children displayed an awareness of the individual nature of the task. They went on to embellish their appropriation of the task, however, with playful moving of chairs and arguing about copying.

In yet another example of literacy homework, the teachers introduced an elaborate literacy project in late May, about one month before the end of the school year. In this project the children were asked to select their favorite short storybook from many that they had read during meeting time over the course of the year and made one photocopy of each book. The children were to take the books home and read them with their parents. They could also color in the pictures, and beginning in the first week of June, they could read their books to the rest of the class during meeting time if they wished to do so. Of the 17 children who attended school regularly in June, 10 read their books during meeting time. The teachers helped the children who had problems and encouraged discussion of the stories during the meetings. They made a special effort to include in the discussion the children who chose not to read their books.

Visits to the Elementary School

Perhaps the most obvious and important priming events related to the coming transition to first grade were the two visits in mid-May to the nearby elementary school that most of the children would attend in the next school year. As we noted in Chapter 2, Bill accompanied the children and teachers on these trips, and we videotaped the activities. During the first visit we were met by the school principal, who gave us a tour of the art, science, and music labs, the playground, the gymnasium, and the cafeteria. We then spent some time in a first-grade classroom whose teacher was the mother of one of the children from our preschool group.

On our second visit we were met by the fifth-grade teachers and students, who took us to their classrooms. In September the preschool children would join one of four new first-grade groups, which would be taught by the current fifth-grade teachers. The older children took the preschoolers under their wings and led them to their desks, showed them their work, and told them all about their classes and their teachers. The preschoolers were thrilled by the attention. The older children, in turn, experienced these visits as a priming event preparing them for leaving the school and the teachers they had worked with for the last 5 years.

On the day following the visits, during meeting time in the preschool, general discussions were held about what the children had observed and learned. They had the opportunity to ask questions and talk about any concerns, fears, or curiosities about the coming transition. The discussions covered a wide range of topics: that there were separate desks for each child, with the teachers' desk at the front; that there would be no opportunities to nap at midday; that there would be less time for play and more time for work; that there would be a lot of homework; that there was a gymnasium; and that the toilets were separated by gender and were different from those in the preschool. Finally, several children mentioned their older siblings and things that the siblings had told them about elementary school.

The trips to the elementary school clearly served as important priming events, as the reality of the transition was brought fully to life. In the discussions some children stated that they were eager to enter the first grade, but all expressed some concerns and worries, which the teachers tried to ease. There was also some discussion about several children who would go to another elementary school, and thus would not be with their friends from preschool.

Near the end of one of the discussions Sandra composed a little song: "I want to stay in preschool and not go to first grade." She smiled as she sang, knowing that this was not possible but still communicating her regret at moving on to the next stage in her life.

Teachers' Concerns About the Transition

Although regrets about leaving the preschool such as those expressed by Sandra were viewed as normal by the teachers, they expressed concern about how some of the children would adjust to the first grade. We discuss the teachers' overall evaluation of the last year of preschool and their concerns about the transition of each child in Chapter 5, where we present results from interviews with the teachers, parents, and children. Here, though, we discuss teacher concerns expressed in activities in the preschool classroom near the end of the school year.

The teachers' greatest concerns centered around the more structured tasks of elementary school and the need for the children to sit still for long periods and pay attention to instructions and lessons. In meeting times during the last 6 weeks, the teachers often did not simply accept answers or discussions from the most active children, as they had done earlier in the year. Instead they often asked, "Why is it always Marina and Luciano? What do you think, Michela? How about you, Mario?" In fact, the teachers told us that even though all the children participated regularly, some had grown accustomed to two or three children speaking for the group. The teachers were concerned that a few children were letting these leaders do their thinking for them and were not paying careful attention.

In one meeting, the teachers told the children about two upcoming events and gave them papers about the activities to take home to their parents. Then they asked the group about the planned events and what they were to tell their parents. Many hands shot up, and a few children began to shout out answers, but the teachers quieted the shouters and called first on Michela and then on Angelo. Both of these children had been sitting quietly; both failed to answer, eventually saying they did not know. The teachers pointed out that they would be expected to know the answers in the first grade and needed to pay attention.

Later Bill talked with Giovanna and remarked that Angelo (who was seated next to him) seemed to know the answers because he mumbled them when the teachers called on Michela. Bill said that Angelo seemed afraid to volunteer what he knew. Giovanna responded that even if he had listened and knew the answer, he would need to speak up and display his knowledge in the first grade.

CONCLUSION

In this chapter we have provided detailed descriptions of routine activities in the school culture at Giuseppe Verdi. We could see that these everyday activities, discussions, and projects built a strong collective culture in the school among the teachers, children, and parents. We also described a number of projects and activities in the final months of the school year that prepared or primed the children for their coming transition to first grade. The most obvious priming activities were the visits to the elementary school. However, several other projects and activities involving literacy development, homework assignments, and reminding children of the need to pay attention in group instruction also served as priming events.

In the next chapter we consider the routines and priming events in the children's peer culture in the preschool. Here we will see the importance of the children's appropriation, use, and refinement of elements of the school culture in their own peer routines. We will also see how in their own peer activities the children begin to anticipate the changes they will encounter in their school lives and relations with peers when they make the transition to first grade.

CHAPTER 4

Sharing, Growing, and Anticipating Change: Priming Events in the Peer Culture

After spending 3 years together in the preschool, the children had produced a rich and complex peer culture. They were very happy to have Bill enter their group because it made them feel special, especially compared to the other 5-year-old group at Giuseppe Verdi preschool. In fact, Bill was in the group (called the 5Bs) only for about a week when he overheard several of the kids telling some of the members of the other 5-year-old group, "Bill is in our class!"

We can see the strong bonds of the group by returning to the celebration of Carnevale that we discussed in Chapter 1. During the party when the kids were all singing and dancing in costume, everyone was also throwing streamers. A group of kids from the other 5-year-old group gathered up a large bunch of streamers. When some kids from the 5bs tried to take some of the streamers, they were resisted. This struggle soon turned into a sort of warfare with the children throwing streamers at each other. Soon children from the two groups gathered piles of streamers and tried to protect them from raids from the opposing group.

Luciano and Carlotta asked Bill to help guard the cache of streamers for their group. Of course, there were plenty of streamers for everyone, but this was beside the point as a struggle over controlling as many streamers as possible had emerged between the two groups. Bill soon found himself trying to ward off raiding parties of boys and girls from the other group. Bill was only partially successful as the kids grabbed a bunch of streamers and threw some of them back at him, hitting him in the face. Luciano returned with Carlotta, Angelo, and Renato and praised Bill for doing a good job. Luciano said they would take over now, and the streamer war continued for some time with most of the children from the two 5-year-old groups participating. Bill joined in now and then to defend the group of kids who had adopted him into the play. He found it emotionally satisfying to be an active member of the group.

This event gave Bill a glimpse of the strong peer bonds of the group he had joined. In his observations over time he discovered a rich and vibrant peer culture with complex friendship relations and many fascinating peer routines and activities. We will only touch on this complexity here by discussing the nature of peer relations in the school and some of the main routines in the peer culture. Then we focus on the priming events we identified in the peer culture which prepared the children for the transition to elementary school.

PEER RELATIONS

When we reviewed our field notes of peer interaction, we saw a general structure in who played with whom and how often they played together. We found that the vast majority of the children (15 of the 21 children in the group) concentrated their shared play around several children. Two children (a boy, Michele, and girl, Viola), often played alone and when they did play with others, it was with three or four other children and normally only for brief periods. Michele was mildly autistic and spent much of free play outside riding a bicycle or playing alone, while Viola had missed a great deal of school because of illness and was slow to join back in the peer culture upon her return.

There were three children who played with all the other children to some degree but concentrated their play with a particular close friend. For example, Elisa and Michela were close friends in that they played with each other nearly twice as often as any other children. Mario also concentrated his play with one friend, Angelo. However, unlike Elisa and Michela, Mario and Angelo were not mutually close friends in that Angelo played with many other children as often as he did with Mario.

This pattern of strong group integration and a lack of differentiation into small groups (especially separated by gender) is somewhat surprising for children 5 to 6 years old given previous research (see Berentzen, 1984; Fernie, Kantor, and Whaley, 1995; Gottman, 1986; Ramsey, 1991; Thorne, 1993). This finding may be related to cultural factors, the curriculum of the school, and the fact that the children were together for such a long period from an early age.

Gender Integration and Separation

The curriculum of this and other Italian preschools in which we have observed strongly encouraged gender integration in teacher-directed and group activities. The girls and boys worked comfortably together on long-term projects, jointly debated different points of view, verbally reproduced past events in group discussions, and shared the fun and excitement of field trips. Preferences in regard to activities and playmates in the peer culture frequently crossed gender lines. Overall, in our field notes of peer interaction, 48.6 percent of the episodes were same-gender (25.7 percent all-girl compared to 22.9 percent all-boy) and 51.4 percent were mixed-gender. This pattern of gender preferences in peer play is quite different from previous research of children of this age, most especially for the boys (see Maccoby, 1999; Maccoby & Jacklin, 1987). For example, Maccoby and Jacklin in a longitudinal study found that when the American children they studied were 4.5 years old they spent 47 percent of their playtime with same-sex playmates and at age 6.5 years same-sex play had increased to 67 percent. The mean age of the children in our study was around 5.5 years. Thus, given the trend in Maccoby and Jacklin's data, our findings represent a lower percentage of same-sex play at this age.

However, it must be pointed out that the units of collection in the two studies differ (as they do in many studies of children's play). Maccoby and Jacklin relied on time sampling of 7-minute observations of indoor and outdoor play. They did code the type of play as well as gender makeup, but unlike our use of the interactive episode as a collection unit (see Corsaro, 1985), time sampling always pulls interaction out of its natural context to some degree.

LaFreniere, Strayer, and Gauthier (1984) relied on random time sampling of social exchanges (initiation, action, response sequences) of individual children in their 3-year longitudinal study of Canadian children. They focused specifically on affiliative, agonistic, and altruistic acts. They found that same-sex play increased over age and that same-sex play among 6-year-old boys made up 65 percent of their affiliative activity while the finding was over 60 percent for 6-year-old girls.

Similar findings of gender separation have been reported using a variety of units of collection among kindergarteners and first graders in the United States (for a review of the literature, see Maccoby, 1999; Thorne, 1993). Thorne is unclear about collection units but relied on field notes and observed a good deal of gender separation and what she called "borderwork," where girls and boys played in oppositional ways, for example, chasing games and boys disrupting girls' play, among the kindergarten and first- and second-grade children in her study. She argued that such play should not be seen as mixed-gender since its main purpose is to set and reinforce boundaries between girls and boys.

Our findings of more mixed-gender compared to same-gender play among Italian 5–6-year-olds are best evaluated in line with recent critiques of the work of Maccoby and others that take a dualistic view of boys and girls. In the dualistic perspective it is argued that differing play interests related to gender lead to gender separation in kindergarten and elementary school. Those critical of Maccoby's interpretations point out that the dual or separate culture view is based on research primarily with white middle-class American children and often fails to take important contextual factors related to peer culture into account (Corsaro, 1994; Goodwin, 1998, 2003; Kyratzis, 2001; Thorne, 1993).

In line with Thorne, we feel it is more profitable to explore "the dynamics of different social institutions and situations" in investigating how gender separation and integration occur than in searching for origins or causes (Thorne, 1993, p. 61). In our group there were four possible contextual dynamics involved. First, taking into account the mildly autistic child and the fact that two children missed a great deal of school during our observations, there were eleven girls compared to seven boys available as everyday playmates. Therefore, the boys had fewer alternatives than girls if their general preference was for same-gender playmates. Despite this disparity, however, three of the boys played in all-boy groups in more than 60 percent of the episodes. So something else beyond playmate availability seems to be important.

A second possibility relates to features of the school and peer culture. Some activities were clearly teacher directed and some free choice, but many others had features of both. Often after group meeting time and before outside play, several children worked on art or literacy projects with teachers, others tended to different aspects of the projects without help from the teachers, and still others choose to engage in peer play. Children often rotated in and out of structured activities and free play. Because structured activities usually involved girls and boys, so too did many of the free choice episodes we observed.

A third contributor to the fairly high level of mixed-gender play was that four boys (Angelo, Luciano, Renato, and Valerio) showed no clear pattern of gender preference in their peer play. In fact, Luciano and Renato played more in mixed- compared to same-gender groups. The fact that all of these boys (especially Angelo) were highly involved in the peer culture also contributed to more cross-gender play.

A fourth and more complex factor was the popularity of certain play routines. While boys were more likely to engage in physical play and sports (riding bikes, superhero play, and soccer) and girls frequently played with dolls, another typical gender-typed activity, dramatic role play, had a more complex pattern that blurred gender stereotypes.

In one type of role play the children re-created variety or game programs on television that were very popular in Italy at the time. Several of these programs had central characters of both genders, and during the reenactment of the shows girls and boys liked to take on all the roles. For example, one program centered around a woman gypsy fortune teller. In their play both girls and boys took turns being the fortune teller and enacting her role with a great deal of flair and zest (see Corsaro, 2003).

A second type of role play was more interesting regarding cross-gender play because it involved a blending of two types of traditional themes—domestic family play and animal role play. In several same-gender episodes girls played house using dolls as babies, and the girls also pretended to be domestic animals (especially kitties) as part of or separate from the domestic theme. Boys never engaged in domestic role play in same-gender episodes, but did at times pretend to be animals. The animals they embodied were, however, almost always aggressive ones like lions and wild dogs.

In addition to these gender stereotyped instances, there were many more episodes of a play routine in which a group of girls and boys pretended to be baby and adolescent wild dogs and lions who prowled around, growling and scratching at each other and other children (see Aydt & Corsaro, 2003; Corsaro, 1985, 2003; Evaldsson & Corsaro, 1998). In this type of play there was most often a mother (and less frequently a father) wild animal who was quite severe in disciplining her children for fighting and biting.

These types of play demonstrate the fascination of both boys and girls with the freedom and aggressiveness of animals in their pretend play. Consider the following example from field notes:

> Sandra and Viviana pretend to be a cat and dog and crawl around the play area creating a fantasy. They pretend that they are lost in the woods and are orphan animals. Then Viviana says she is dead. Sandra responds that she cannot talk if she is dead. Viviana, however, counters by arguing that it is her spirit talking, but Sandra says that animals do not have spirits. The girls now move their play to the story book and house area where some toy animals and dolls are stored. The girls bring the toy animals into the play by pretending to eat them. As Sandra pretends to eat a zebra she says, "*Una bella bistecca!* (What a good steak!)

In both these types of role play the children embellished and extended the traditional gender scripts by stretching or plying the adult role frame (Goffman, 1974). This plying of the frame gave the children more control over it and enabled them to move the play in directions that fit certain concerns of the peer culture. Thus boys could be gypsy fortune tellers and girls could be aggressive animals.

Conflict Resolution

The children in this group, like other Italian children we have studied, valued verbal debate and discussion (Corsaro, 1994, 2003; Corsaro & Rizzo,

1988). Italians refer to this type of debate as *discussione*. Such *discussione* was an integral part of the school and peer culture because in such debate the children shared a sense of collective identity, forged friendships, and displayed personal identity. The children were careful, however, to keep the *discussione* from escalating into personal conflict.

Children frequently did this through humor. Often in verbal debates a child who may be losing ground will accuse the other of trying to be the boss or a "know-it-all." For example, several boys were putting away materials they had been playing with before snack time. One boy, Valerio, stops helping and starts giving directions to the others regarding how the materials are to be arranged in the cupboard. At first the others follow his orders, but Daniele complains, telling Valerio, *"Non sei capo di tutto!"* ("You're not the boss of everything!"). All the children laugh, including Valerio who now begins to help the others. Another favorite retort in a debate is to refer to the party with the upper hand as *"professore"* ("professor"), a back-handed compliment indicating that the person is taking on airs.

Undoubtedly, the children have picked up the strategy of using humor to make a point from Italian adults (parents and teachers), who frequently use the tactic to control children's untoward behavior. However, children often extend the strategy in line with aspects of the peer culture. Consider the following example:

> Bill is sitting at a table with several children (Carlotta, Elisa, Mario, Valerio, and Viviana) who are drawing. A discussion escalates briefly as one child calls another a liar, but then things calm down. A bit later there is a struggle over the wastebasket used to catch pencil shavings. Elisa takes the basket and puts it near her, but out of sight under the table. Viviana sees this and says, *"C'era la E-l-is-a"* ("It was Elisa") elongating Elisa. Then Carlotta says, *"Era la c-a-c-c-a!"* ("It was poo-poo") elongating *cac-ca*. This joking around continues with Valerio acting like a little baby and pretending to cry. This leads to a discussion of who is a *"piagnucolone"* ("big crybaby"). Carlotta and Elisa say Valerio and Viviana are. Viviana does not like this and protests. But Elisa persists, chanting, *"Sei una piagnucolona!"* ("You are a crybaby") which is repeated several times by Elisa and Carlotta. Valerio, who does cry a lot, does not deny it and accepts the label. Viviana, however, does not like the idea of being placed in this category with Valerio and protests, but she does not persist and the chanting stops.

In this example a more serious dispute is deflated with humor in Viviana's voicing of Elisa's name and Carlotta's reference to *"cac-ca."* Once the humorous frame is established, the children then discuss a serious issue in the peer culture ("being seen as a crybaby") with Valerio actually accepting the label and Viviana resisting it but not becoming upset.

In some instances humor was not enough to quell conflict, and serious disputes occurred. In many such cases, however, uninvolved children negotiated peace between the warring parties. Consider the following example:

> Luciano, Lorenzo, and Renato are in the outside yard playing with some small toy tractors that Lorenzo has brought to school. Another boy, Alessio, enters the play and asks to use one of the tractors, but he is told to wait by Lorenzo. After waiting for some time, Alessio says the boys are not being fair. He walks over to some girls, Marina and Elisa, who are playing nearby, and complains to them that Lorenzo will not share the tractors. The girls seem excited that Alessio has come to them for help. They call over Carlotta, Stefania, and Federica. The girls get into a huddle and devise a plan to help Alessio. They are very excited and talk about distracting Luciano and grabbing one of the tractors. The girls go over where Luciano, Lorenzo, and Renato are playing, with Alessio following behind. Elisa and Marina go up and begin to push Luciano and Carlotta tries to grab a tractor. Luciano fights off the girls and Lorenzo and Renato protect the tractor from Carlotta. Marina then tells Luciano that she will tell the teacher, Carla, and she runs over to do so. Luciano seems threatened by this and follows after Marina. Marina begins to tell Carla about the problem, but Carla cuts her short. She tells the children they must work it out by themselves. Luciano is somewhat relieved and returns to Lorenzo and Renato. The girls now run off together with Alessio and they say they will try again. They say they are the blue army and that Luciano, Lorenzo, and Renato are the red army. There is also some talk of making peace. However, before they can devise a new plan, it is time to go in for lunch.

This was one of several examples where a small group of children (usually 4 or 5) worked together to try to settle a serious rift among their playmates. In fact, this occurred several times in disputes between Carlotta and Stefania, again with both boys and girls involved in the peace process. In this instance, and in almost all of these cases, a teacher or teachers became aware of the problem, but left the children alone to settle things themselves. The children saw serious conflict between or among their peers as a threat to the strong group identity of the peer culture and worked collaboratively to reduce this threat. In many of these cases the children would beseech the opposing parties to establish "peace" (see Corsaro, 2003; Corsaro & Molinari, 2000a). In the case above the children had not yet reached the point of a peace phase, but this may have occurred if the episode had not been cut short.

PRIMING EVENTS

When the children talked about first grade, they often referred to age: Kids go to elementary school when they are 6 years old. When discussing age and elementary school, the children frequently referred to the experiences of older siblings. These discussions often were embedded in routines of the peer culture.

Discussioni

As we discussed earlier the children frequently engaged in discussions and debates. In the following example, a debate about who is responsible for a broken pencil evolves into a stylized and (in the end) playful exchange of threats that is related to the children's connection of age with elementary school.

> An argument develops between Marina and Angelo. Supposedly Marina said Angelo had broken Elisa's pencil. Bill did not actually hear this since Marina left the area and supposedly told Elisa this, who also was no longer in the area. In any case, Marina has now returned and Angelo has followed her, saying she is a liar and that her nose will grow longer than Pinocchio's for telling lies. Marina denies that she lied, and after several exchanges the children start making threats. Angelo says his brother in first grade will beat up Marina. Then Marina says her brother in second grade will beat up Angelo's brother in first grade. Angelo now says that his brother in third grade will beat up Marina's brother in second grade. Angelo still seems to be taking it all pretty seriously, but Marina starts to smile, and she is laughing when she says that her cousin in fourth grade will beat up Angelo's brother in third grade. Angelo smiles at this and the dispute ends.

Some of the threats made in this example could actually be carried out because both Angelo and Marina have a brother in elementary school. Reality clearly was being stretched, however, as the threats became more fanciful. In fact, the children's engagement in what Flaherty (1984, p. 75) calls "reality play" ("the harmless toying with the cultural or interpersonal expectations apropos" to the contingencies in a given episode of interaction) is important in several respects.

First, the serious concern about lying to a friend was addressed in the everyday routine of *discussione*. The use of stock phrases and references such as the length of Pinocchio's nose are common in *discussione*, and reflect the appreciation of stylized debate among Italians as opposed to more serious dispute.

Second, the use of the more subtle humor or "reality play" (the impossibility of having siblings at every grade level) lightened the seriousness of the discussion even more, and deftly connected a typical peer spat to the children's ongoing concern about ending their time together as a group and moving to a new school. Thus the children's thinking about age in terms of where they are and where they are going in the educational system is anchored in the everyday routines of peer culture.

In addition to age, the children often talked of elementary school as a place where children did lessons and had homework (*i compiti*). Here again, siblings were important. Sofia pointed out that her sister had little time for fun during the Easter break because she had so much "*i compiti*." Thus one aspect of the social representation of the first grade was clearly that it would be a place more for work than for play, as compared to preschool.

Interest in Literacy Activities

The most notable aspect of priming in the peer culture occurred in the last 2 months of preschool. In this period the children displayed a keen interest in literacy activities during free play and other routines of peer culture (see Corsaro & Nelson, 2003). This interest was first apparent in relation to a routine that had developed between Bill and the children. Early on in the research, the kids asked Bill about what he was writing in the small notebook in which he recorded field notes. He responded that he wrote down things they said so that he would remember them later. Also, he often showed the notebook to the children, telling them that most of what he wrote was in English. The children inspected the book, and during the first 2 months of observation they often asked to draw pictures in it. Beginning in the third month, however, they began to print and write things in the notebook.

The children usually printed their names or the names of their friends or siblings. They also began to print the names of the things they drew, such as "tree" or "house." In June the children printed and wrote in the notebook every day. During the last 2 months of the school term 16 of the 17 children who attended school regularly printed or wrote something in Bill's notebook.

The children's interest in literacy was also apparent in other peer activities. In their drawings they often reproduced words or phrases from stories read to them. They also discussed how they would read and write in first grade. The following example captures the complexity of some literacy activities:

> During free play several children want to print their names in Bill's notebook:
>   MARINA
>   STEFANIA

FEDERICA

Luciano is now writing a letter to his sister as Sofia sits nearby. Sofia tells Bill to write what Luciano is doing in his notebook. So Bill does so in Italian and shows it to her:

LUCIANO SCRIVE UNA LETTERA ALLA SUA SORELLINA. (Luciano writes a letter to his little sister).

Luciano then suggests that Sofia also write a letter to his sister which she does with Luciano's help. It reads:

CARA LAURA, (Dear Laura,)

TANTI BACIONI DA SOFIA LUCIANO E DA Bill. (Many big kisses from Sofia Luciano and from Bill).

This example is interesting not only because it demonstrates the children's skills in writing, but also because it displays their awareness of the interest of the researcher in their literacy skills. The children not only inscribe data into Bill's notebook, but tell him what they think is important about the peer culture to include in his notes (Corsaro & Nelson, 2003).

In addition to printing in Bill's notebook and also printing words during free play, the children in some cases had conversations where they speculated about elementary school. For example, Stefania and Sofia were playing with Legos and began to talk about elementary school. Stefania said they would write in cursive rather than print. Sofia wondered what their new teachers would be like and what other new things they would have to learn.

It is not surprising that some children begin to read and write before entering the first grade and see these as skills they will develop further in elementary school. Nor is it remarkable that such activities prepare the children for the transition. Our point, however, is not simply that children begin and practice literacy activities before entering formal schooling. Rather, we argue that these collective activities are first produced in interaction with the teachers in projects intended to develop an orientation to literacy and then are appropriated and used collectively by the children in their own peer culture. In the process we see the projective representations about future activities in the first grade originate in collective activities in the preschool (Corsaro & Molinari, 2000b).

Anticipation of Changes in Friendships

Finally, this relationship between collective actions and children's representations of future transitions was also apparent in children's anticipation of possible changes in friendship relations. The children understood that they would not be able to stay together as a group in the first grade because they would be separated into four classes. Surprisingly, the children rarely mentioned this coming change. Several children, however, expressed concern that two of their playmates (Angelo and Daniele) would be attending a different school. The children seemed to have a clearer understanding of this coming change because both Angelo and Daniele talked about it frequently. Furthermore, Angelo participated in the visit to the local elementary school even though he would not attend the school in the fall. During discussions about the school visits in meeting time several children including Angelo remarked that when they returned to the school in the fall, Angelo would not be with them. Here again we see how shared collective actions in priming events nurture the development of representations about future change.

CONCLUSION

In this chapter and Chapter 3 we have provided thick descriptions of important features of the school and peer cultures at Giuseppe Verdi. We then went on to show how both formal priming events (like the visits to the elementary school) and informal ones embedded in the everyday routines of the peer culture affected the children's perspectives and prepared them for the coming transition to first grade. We could see this in the nature of the activities themselves and the children's own talk about their futures with the teachers and peers.

These priming events can be seen metaphorically as "constructing a bridge." Most of the major transitions in children's lives involve movement across space or territory; and therefore, the image of a bridge is a good one. In priming events in the school culture and peer culture in the preschool, the children, with adults and one another, collectively constructed the initial part of the bridge that moved them beyond their everyday routines and interactions. It is a bridge of separation from the present that juts out or projects into the future near this key transition point in their lives. However, the bridge was not completed in the collective actions of priming events, and it takes the children only so far into their futures. With their initial collective construction of the bridge, children moved into what the anthropologist Victor Turner calls a period or space of liminality—a place and time "betwixt and between the positions assigned and arranged by law, custom, convention, and ceremonial" (1974, p. 95).

In the next chapter we consider the children's lives in this period of liminality by examining interviews conducted with parents and teachers near the end of the children's last year in preschool and additional interviews with parents, children, and teachers during the first months of elementary school. In this way we gain insight into the children's, parents', and teachers' perspectives of the transition process.

CHAPTER 5

The Coming Transition to Elementary School: Perceptions of Teachers, Children, and Parents

One night, just a few days after the end of the school year at Giuseppe Verdi preschool, we invited the two preschool teachers, Giovanna and Carla, for dinner. After dinner we interviewed them together about their last year in the school, the activities they organized, and their relationships with the children. When we asked which aspects of their jobs were most satisfying for them, they both answered synchronously:

> We love to be able to establish relationships with the children based on affection and confidence, because this is the basis on which we can realize everything else, and also relationships with the parents based on collaboration and trust, because this means that they appreciate us as teachers who contribute to their children's development.

In this quote we see the close relationship that has been established among the teachers, children, and parents over 3 years together in the preschool. With their time together now ended, all members of this community reflect on and appreciate their time together, but they also look to the future.

This chapter focuses on the teachers', children's, and parents' perceptions about the coming transition to elementary school. All these participants in the transition consider this event from different points of view, which we studied through in-depth interviews carried out on two occasions, one just before the summer vacation and the second a few months after the transition had been made. We will also reflect on some occasions of verbal exchanges among the children and between the children and the teachers, developed both in the peer and in the school culture in the preschool, which highlight their representations and projections into the future.

The material presented in this chapter allows us to stress the importance of the reconstruction of past experiences with reference to future concerns, and for this reason it can be useful to refer to a much neglected phenomenon in the study of socialization, *rites of passage*. The best known work on rites of passage is that of van Gennep, who characterized them in this general way:

> For groups, as well as for individuals, life itself means to separate and to be reunited, to change form and condition, to die and to be reborn. It is to act and to cease, to wait and rest, and to begin acting again, but in a different way (1960, p. 189).

Van Gennep extended earlier anthropological work on rites of passage, which tended to be primarily descriptive, and focused on classifying specific rites or ceremonies of different cultures. He was not so much interested in particular rites, but rather in their significance or relative position within ceremonial wholes (Kimball, 1960). Thus he distinguished between rites of separation, rites of transition, and rites of incorporation. However, he noted that in specific instances the three types are not always equally important or elaborated.

For our purposes, van Gennep's analysis of rites of passage is overly functional and too individualistic. Contrary to his conceptualization, we emphasize that the rites are primarily collective actions performed in groups and normally performed in public with audiences playing an important role, although they may have private elements. Still, van Gennep's distinction between rites of separation and incorporation is important because it captures collective and public elements of groups or cohorts of individuals ending their active membership in one local culture and entering and becoming part of the customary routines of another.

Here we discuss the children's and adults' perceptions of the transition, following the general rites' distinction of preliminal (separation) and liminal (margin), while taking up the postliminal (incorporation) in Chapter 8. Children face the separation (at the end of preschool) and incorporation rites (at the beginning of elementary school) within the collective group's cultures, while the liminal period, occurring in the time between the other two, is spent with the families (for additional discussion of liminality, see Turner, 1974).

REPRESENTATIONS OF PRIMING EVENTS

One of the main aims of working with interviews directed to different people who are part of children's lives is to acquire a clearer understanding of the ways in which contributions from the various environments of the children are complementary, and the ways in which they are different. The link between action and representations is particularly important because parents, teachers, peers, and siblings are part of the children's lives during the transition period, participate actively in the changes that occur, and contribute to decisions that bear on various aspects of priming activities. In this sense we are studying social representations, highlighting how parents, teachers, and peers share knowledge and thereby constitute their common reality and culture, and how they transform their ideas into the practice of everyday life with the children. In particular, we are interested in the microgenetic process of social representations (Duveen & Lloyd, 1990) as organized in social interactions, when people meet, talk, discuss, and resolve conflicts. Our focus is summed up in the words of Rogoff, Baker-Sennet, and Matusov: how people together transform their responsibility in participation in sociocultural activities rather than on how external mental knowledge and skills [are] internalized or how the social world influences the individual (1994, p. 369).

Teachers' Representations

In our interview with the preschool teachers, Giovanna and Carla, we noted that their response reflected a long, shared experience with preschool children. We asked them to reflect on the last year of school in terms of priming events and make predictions regarding the children's adjustment in the elementary school. The general idea that the teachers expressed when reflecting about priming was that their main aim was not to teach the children to read and write, but to help them develop some prerequisites, such as the ability to listen carefully, to comprehend the meaning of a story, and to respect the general rules of conversations. As Carla stated,

> For us, more than teaching to read and write, there are skills that . . . even if some of the children in our group have not learned how to read, this they will inevitably be able to do in elementary school. It is more important to establish all the prerequisites, those of paying attention, of comprehension.

During the interview, we discovered in the teachers' narratives that the development of the prerequisites for literacy abilities was not limited to the important activities that we described in the previous chapter (long-term projects, such as "light and dark" and "*Wizard of Oz*"), but started in the first year of work with this group of children, when they were 3 years old. That year, the teachers spent a lot of time reading short books, and discussing with the group of children the meaning of the words and the sequence of the stories. In the second year, when the children were 4, they organized a long-term project centered in literacy. They based this project on the book

The Knights of the Round Table, not an easy book for children of that age, and they worked both on the physical setting of the story—making a three-dimensional castle, costumes for the dames and the knights, a throne—and on the reading and comprehension of the story—reading chapters of the book every day, stimulating discussions about the story, creating dramas concerning the story. The entire project lasted 3 months.

Reflecting on the children's transition to elementary school, Carla noted a number of differences between the two school systems:

> In my opinion, elementary school is very different because the teachers have to evaluate the children on a specific measure—they have to say if they have reached, partially reached, or not reached the results—and this is the main preoccupation of a teacher. For this reason, they probably do not have time to do other activities, while in our job there is more flexibility, that makes us and the children very relaxed.

When asked to describe the children and anticipate their reactions to the transition, the teachers noted that the children differed as far as security and confidence with new situations. They mainly described the children with reference to two sets of behaviors. A number of children were already very confident about themselves and in their relationships with peers and adults when they entered preschool, while other children changed a lot from the time they entered, when they were very shy, reserved, and insecure. The teachers described this change as an "incredible transformation," an important growth. As noted in Chapter 3, the teachers expressed some fears about the transition to elementary school only for a few children, given the fact that they still behaved in an insecure way, and tended to follow the others (both peers and adults) instead of trying to make suggestions and participate directly in both the school and peer cultures.

If we agree with Pianta and Cox (1999a) that enhancing relationships between children and teachers constitutes an important supportive factor especially in the first school years, then these teachers have done a great job in helping the children face the important transition from preschool to elementary school. It is also clear that the Italian system of 3 years of publicly supported preschool with children staying in the same group, usually with the same teachers, is a highly innovative and important factor in the successful transition to elementary school.

Children's Representations

We did not interview the children before the end of preschool. However, we were able to gain insight on how they look ahead to their coming transition to elementary school through the analysis of some conversations that we audiotaped during the 2 months that preceded the end of the school term.

In Chapter 4 we discussed how priming events in the peer culture were often considered with reference to two factors, that is, the children's increasing age and interactions with older siblings. The references to these two factors became very relevant and frequent especially in the last weeks before the end of preschool, when children were well aware of the coming separation from the group of classmates with whom they had shared 3 years of life.

Consider the following conversation that was audiotaped just 10 days before the end of the school year. This exchange developed among a small group of children who were working on a present for Giovanna, who had been absent from school for several weeks of family leave so that she and her husband could travel to another country to adopt two children.

> Several children are sitting at a work table making some drawings for the present. Luciano had criticized Viviana's work.
>
> "It is not true, it is not true, you are a big liar, see!" Viviana says to Luciano. "You are a liar."
>
> "Liar you!" responds Luciano.
>
> "But you are always saying that it is my fault, never anyone else, never anyone els-e-e-e," says Viviana in a whiny voice. "Why always me?"
>
> Carla, who overhears the dispute from the other side of the room, says, "Viviana must stop whining, because now she is a big girl. I don't want to see her crying again, you can talk, not whine."
>
> "Otherwise you are an *asilo nido* [program for toddlers] child," declares Stefania.
>
> "You can discuss while talking, without whining," adds Carla.
>
> "Only the young kids cry," says Stefania. "I understand my sister, she was just born, but you are a big girl, Viviana, you are older than me."
>
> "But excuse me, but . . ." starts Viviana.
>
> "You are 6! Do you realize? You are 6 years old!" says Stefania.
>
> "That's right," says Angelo, "my brother, do you know that he is 7, and he still sucks his finger?"
>
> "Hah!" Stefania laughs.
>
> "Mario is a little boy," says Viviana.
>
> "But did you ever see him cry?" retorts Angelo. "I have never seen him!"
>
> "Yes, he is a big boy, you are a small girl, always whining," says Stefania to Viviana.
>
> "Stop it, Stefania," says Carla, now coming to Viviana's defense.

This discussion is focused on the children's interest in combining behaviors and related developmental steps. The first exchanges arise after a dispute between Luciano and Viviana that upsets Viviana. The teacher, Carla, tries to stop the dispute interpreting Viviana's behavior as not in line with her age: Being a big girl, she cannot whine after verbal disputes with classmates. Just after Carla's intervention, another girl, Stefania, makes reference to the *asilo nido* children who are allowed, since they are very young, to react by whining when they have a problem. Stefania later reinforces her position stating that her newborn sister also can cry, but not Viviana, who is even older then Stefania herself (Viviana is already 6 years old, while Stefania will be 6 in a few months). Angelo now enters the discussion and introduces a further example of a discrepancy between age and behavior, referring to his brother, who is 7 and still sucks his finger which makes Stefania laugh. Viviana now tries to defend herself by referring to another classmate who is a young boy (Mario is actually the youngest boy in the group), but this reference is inconsistent, as Angelo and Stefania note when arguing that Mario behaves as a big boy and never cries. The exchange is then closed by Carla sensing that the point has been made and protecting Viviana from further criticism.

This short discussion allows the children to share representations of the coming transition. In fact, they refer to several aspects that make them aware of developmental changes, especially the fact that behaviors that were allowed in different ages or different contexts (for example, in the Italian *asilo nido*), are not consistent with the age range of preschool children. This activity can be considered as a priming event because the children make reference to different contexts and different points in the life cycle as having specific characteristics. In this way they anticipate the idea that in elementary school they will have to behave in ways consistent with present and future contexts and their increasing age.

As already discussed in Chapter 3, the visit to the elementary school was an important priming event within the school culture. The conversations that preceded and followed the visits are also important examples of how the children's collective reflection on priming events helps the social construction of knowledge.

Consider the morning meeting that took place between one of the teachers, Carla, and the children just a couple of hours before the first visit to the school.

"At 11 o'clock we will go and visit the elementary school," says Carla. "We'll go and see how it is, some of you already know how it is."

"I know, I know!" shout several children.

"You must learn how to write," declares Carlotta.

"How is an elementary school a place where you can learn how to read and write?" asks Carla.

"There are classes with teachers," says Carlotta.

"With some desks," adds Sandra.

"Ah, that's true," says Carla, "they are called *classi*, not *sezioni* [as in preschool].

"We said that there are the classes: many classes or a few classes?" asks Carla.

"Many!" shout the children in unison.

"With the desks, with the chairs," adds Carla.

"With the teachers' desks," says Angelo.

"And what are they called, the teachers' desks?" asks Carla.

"Table?" guesses Angelo.

"Little table? Big table? Round table?" ask several children.

"No, no, no, its name is *cattedra*," points out Carla, "the big table that the teachers use."

This conversation is priming children for the entrance into the new school, which has some differences as compared to the preschool with which they are very familiar. The way Carla directs the conversation is organized to stress these differences, so that the children will not be struck by them and feel uncomfortable.

During the visit, the children were joined by the fifth-grade children who were in their last year of elementary school. The fifth-grade children were acting as guides because their teachers would be the teachers for the first graders in the following year. One group of children was taken to the drawing lab, and they were asked to make a drawing of a friend, to leave as a present in the school. Consider part of the conversation that took place a few days after the visit between the teacher, Carla, and the preschool children.

"And you, Luciano, what did you draw as a present for the school?"

"I drew my sister with two ponytails," responds Luciano.

"It's true, you drew Laura with two ponytails. And you, Michela, what did you draw?" asks Carla.

"A girl," answers Michela.

"And you, Carlotta?" asks Carla.

"I drew a girl, and on the edge there was some grass with the sun in the sky," says Carlotta.

"And you, Angelo?"

"I drew a friend who is in that school."

"Can I say a something?" asks Elisa. "That you, Angelo, didn't draw your brother, because your brother is not in that elementary school, and also my cousin, then if you get to know him . . ."

"Will your cousin also go to [name of another elementary school] that Angelo will attend?" asks Carla.

"Maurizio is the name of my cousin," says Elisa.

"When I will be 6, I will start Class IA," says Angelo.

"It is possible that Maurizio will also go to Class IA, and maybe you will meet," says Carla.

This exchange is very interesting, because the children take the occasion to raise a problem that is very relevant for them in this period of life: While the majority of the group will go to the same elementary school (the one they visited), a few children will go to different schools. They all know that in elementary school they will be divided into four class groups, but they are also aware that they will have the opportunity to play together and to meet every day, independently of the class they will be enrolled in. At the same time, they will probably not see their current peers and friends who will be going to a different school at least not on a daily basis. Angelo, a very popular child, is one such friend; his older brother is already attending a different elementary school.

During the visit to the school, Angelo chose to make a drawing of "a friend who is in that school," and this statement is interpreted by Elisa as a wish not to draw his brother, because he is attending a different school. Elisa then tries to propose a connection between Angelo and the rest of the group, using her cousin Maurizio, who will probably go to the same school as Angelo and perhaps will be in his same class. This example shows that the children are anticipating very insightfully the future changes in their lives. Furthermore, they work collectively in the familiar routine of a morning discussion to make sense of present and future experiences. We see here an excellent example of children's agency, priming, and processes of interpretive reproduction.

Parents' Representations

The first set of interviews with a subgroup of eight parents who agreed to participate was collected in the final 2 months of preschool. In some cases both mothers and fathers participated in the interview, while in others, when they wished, only one parent was present.

The first impression that we gained from the interviews was that the parents' representations in many ways complemented the children's discussions in the school. The following example with Elisa's mother and father clearly illustrates the value of sharing school experiences within the family.

Father: For example, yesterday evening we went to visit my father who lives down this road. On the way back she did not want to take the shortest way, but she said, "Let's go and take a trip." We went around one block. There is a school there, what's the name?

Mother: It's our school, where we shall go.
Father: Elementary school.
Mother: Elementary school.
Father: We passed in front of it, and then she told me, "You know, daddy, I went to see the school where I will go next year."

Here Elisa took the occasion of a short trip as an opportunity to share with her father her earlier visit to the school, and used it as a means to discuss the coming change with him. In this way, the school and the family hold complementary views about the importance of the earlier visit to the elementary school as a priming event.

Parents expressed different feelings about the possible difficulties their children might encounter in the transition. Some parents emphasized that their children were ready because the preschool teachers had worked hard to prepare them for the coming transition. In some cases, however, the parents' words also revealed hesitations and even regret in realizing that their children were growing up and moving into a new period of their lives.

Other parents communicated more specific concerns about the transition. Luciano's mother, for example, feared that her son might face problems in elementary school because "he will have to sit still, be quiet, and listen to the teacher." She was quite aware that he had been prepared by the preschool teachers, that the visit to the school was important as a priming event, and therefore that he knew how it would be. Yet, she was not able to link this image completely to the actual practices and demands of elementary school. As we will see in Chapter 8, Luciano's first-grade teacher does report some adjustment problems that are related to, but go beyond, his mother's concerns.

The parents' representations of priming events were centered on a main topic, that is, the reference to siblings as the most important agents helping in the transition. Parents frequently referred to the importance of siblings, noting that having older siblings could make transitions much smoother. Siblings were often linked to the question of learning how to read and write before starting elementary school. Parents with more than one child often pointed out that the younger child frequently took advantage of opportunities to participate in older siblings' lives. Irene's parents, for example, anticipated that their daughter would have an easy transition because her sister had prepared her well.

Interviewer: You mean that she already has an image of primary school, a very clear one?
Father: Yes, probably she built it on the basis of her sister's ideas. Thus she already lives this thing, that in school you have homework, that

you read, that you write, that teachers sometimes make children be quiet, sometimes you cannot play so much, that it is tiring.

Interviewer: Is she worried about this?

Father: No, on the contrary, she is looking forward so much to going to elementary school. In fact she is already studying, she can read and write. Contrary to what happened to her sister, who was not able to read and write when she started school, Irene can read and write.

Irene's father is aware that representations of the coming transition to first grade concerned various aspects of school: homework, reading, writing, being quiet, and limited play. These aspects were the same as those which were constructed in the children's culture during participation in routines in preschool. When referring to the possible disadvantages of their older daughter (who was the first child in the family), this father gave more emphasis to literacy abilities. He felt that when the abilities to read and write are not well developed, this seems to cause the most problems for the oldest child in the family when beginning first grade.

Overall, the parents were more concerned than the preschool teachers about the importance of well-developed literacy skills. The mother of Sonia, for example, emphasized in the interview her child's competencies in literacy, and she stressed that these competencies were developed by the child in complete autonomy from the teachers' or the parents' requests.

> I never pushed her to learn, she started to be interested in reading when she was 3. In the evenings she used to ask, "What's written here?" when my husband and I were reading. Then she wanted to learn the alphabet; we wrote it and she copied it. Then she started to read a few words, on the advertisements in the streets, on the shops, and she was always asking why, why.

The differences among children in literacy skills were clear to the parents, and constituted a problem for those who did not show such interest. In some cases, as seen here in this interview with Renato's parents, the explanation referred to the role of older siblings as priming agents.

Mother: He is a bit worried.

Interviewer: But is he worried because he can see that other children can write?

Mother: Yes, I think that is the reason, because he noticed that other kids . . .

Father: He is a bit behind the others, but not all of them. Those children are too far in advance, in my opinion.

Mother: Then they have brothers or sisters going to school, and therefore are more motivated.

Father: His things now is toys; these things interest him most. If he does something it is because you tell him to do it; otherwise his favorite activity is to play.

In this example, the parents minimized the importance of knowing how to read and write before starting elementary school. Instead they argued that it was normal, given their child's age, that he still enjoyed play and preferred it to beginning to learn to read and write. Even so, they admitted that their son's limitation in literacy skills was their major preoccupation concerning the transition.

Since parents were not participants in the everyday routines of the preschool, their representations of their children's literacy abilities were based primarily on observations of their children's performance in products brought from the school, in their children's reading and writing at home, and on their children's reports of their own literacy skills in comparison with those of their peers. Therefore, the parents' representations were not tied to action and were instead more abstract evaluations of overall literacy ability. Literacy, in the parents' representations, centered around a broad judgment of competence in which their children and their peers in the preschool were placed into one of two groups: those who generally know how to read and write and those who do not.

THE LIMINAL PERIOD BETWEEN PRESCHOOL AND ELEMENTARY SCHOOL

As noted earlier, the transition from one school to another in all Western cultures consist of three passages: the "separation," which is the final part of the old school year; the "incorporation" into the culture of the new school; and the "liminal" passage, that is, the period between the other two. These three passages complete the metaphor of the bridge between preschool and elementary school.

For the children we studied, the period of liminality coincided with summer vacation, which was spent with their families but with no, or few, contacts with class friends and teachers. It is not an easy period, the children miss the daily collective routines with teachers and peers, and are projected into a future that is somehow unknown and mysterious.

During the last days in preschool, children were often anticipating this important border, which means separation from their old peers and incorporation into new groups of children. The following conversation was audiotaped just a few days before the school's end, and it followed the dispute between Viviana and Luciano that we discussed earlier. It is in line with our earlier discussion in Chapter 4 of the children's attempts to settle their own disputes and make peace.

> "In a month we will not see each other any more," notes Viviana.
> "Let's make peace, Vivi," suggests Luciano.
> "Yeah," replies Viviana.
> "*Pace, pace, carote, patate* (Peace, peace, carrots, potatoes)," chant Viviana and Luciano in unison.
> "Yes, very good," says Bill who is sitting at the table with them.
> "Eh, you said that you would never forgive her," says Angelo to Luciano.
> "And then . . . then I was tired of it," responds Luciano.
> "And also that she . . ."
> "*Pace, pace, carote, patate*," Luciano repeats.

The exchange starts with Viviana expressing her worry about the coming separation from friends. Luciano then suggests they "make peace", and they do so with their little rhyme. Angelo then speaks up and notes Luciano's inconsistency with previous statements. But as the school year is about to end, Luciano says he is tired of the conflict. He again produces the rhyme of peace in the singsong chant of the *cantilena*, which is often heard in the peer culture of Italian preschool children (see Corsaro, 2003, 2005).

Preschool finished the last day of June. It was a very emotional day, during which everybody exchanged presents. The children gave drawings to Bill, the teachers bought ice cream for the children, and the children exchanged small objects among themselves. Sofia who was noticeably upset is calmed and very touched when Luciano gave her a kite that he made during a school activity and that he knew Sofia liked a lot.

We interviewed the children and their parents again in the fall. Part of these interviews consisted of questions related to how the children spent the time before the start of elementary school. Some of the children behaved in this period in ways that showed their worries over the new school, their new classmates, and the new teachers. Here is part of the interview with Stefania and her mother.

Mother: She was worried. Were you worried last summer?
Stefania: Yes, all of a sudden, really at the end of preschool, at the end really.
Interviewer: Yes, in the summer.
Stefania: When I had to go to elementary school, suddenly I stopped eating, I didn't want to eat, even soup, which I liked very much, I

used to finish it, now I could not finish it, not even the peas, which I loved.
Interviewer: Perhaps you were very worried, very upset.
Stefania: Not even the peas, and the soup, nothing.

In this discussion, Stefania states that her anxiety and fears about the start of first grade made her reject her favorite foods. Carlotta's mother reported a conversation with her child, who questioned the necessity of going to school and discussed the possibility of staying at home at least when she was ill:

> The last week before the school's starting she said that she didn't want to go to school. "No, no, I don't want to go to elementary school." She refused school, who knows why, we had talked a lot about it, then just before the start she said she didn't want to go. I said, "Listen, if you don't go to school, then the policemen will come and ask you why"; and she replied, "What about if I am sick?" "Yes, you can be sick for some days, but not forever!"

Then school started, and children reached the third part of the bridge, and incorporated new values, rules, and relations in their cultures.

CONCLUSION

In this chapter we have presented the adults' and children's representations about the transition from preschool to elementary school, representations that emerged both from interviews and from discussions in preschool. The data show that in some cases the representations are shared while in others they are not. For example, we found that parents and children shared a sense of the importance of age and siblings in their representations of the coming transition, while parents and teachers differed in their judgments of literacy competence and the importance of literacy skills as priming the transition. While parents viewed literacy in the bimodal categories of general competence or incompetence, preschool teachers saw literacy as a complex set of activities that serve as prerequisites for actual skills. In many ways, these differences existed because the parents' representations did not develop as part of the routine collective actions in daily life.

PART III

Studying and Deepening Friendships at Giacomo Puccini Elementary School

Rules, Lessons, and Literacy: Developing Membership in the First-Grade School Culture

Shortly before the start of classes in the elementary school, we met with the first-grade teachers; there were two teachers for each of the four new first-grade classes at Giacomo Puccini elementary school. Because of our previous work in the preschool and our focus on transition, the teachers were quite interested in our research. Transition issues were very important to them, especially because the group of children that made up their first-grade class would be in their charge for the entire 5 years of elementary school.

At the meeting we learned the assignments of students for each class and also heard about the difficulty of the decisions. As pointed out in Chapter 1, because of a demographic quirk, twice as many girls as boys (50 girls and 25 boys) were entering the first grade (in higher grades the size of the group rose to about 80 with about the same gender mix). The teachers faced certain other constraints as well, including the placement of students with special needs, but worked hard to ensure that no class would contain more than the 2 to 1 ratio of girls to boys.

We agreed on a schedule whereby Bill would visit the school 4 days a week, spending one morning in each of the four classrooms (Prima A, Prima B, Prima C, and Prima D). As we discussed earlier, the Italian preschool and elementary school have a common organizational structure in that the children are placed into groups with two teachers, and normally remain in these groups with at least one of those teachers during their entire time in the institution (3 years in preschool and 5 years in elementary school). In addition, the particular classes are part of a larger community: In the elementary school, for example, four first-grade groups belong to a community of several such groups that include the second, third, fourth, and fifth grade. Thus, given their experiences in preschool, the children can easily see and understand the

73

place of their new group in the organizational structure of the elementary school. The new and different features for the children, when they enter elementary school, are the particular children who are their new classmates, their teachers, and the more advanced nature of their educational activities. Also for the first time there was a somewhat mysterious person of great importance: the director of the elementary school. She came to visit all the classrooms on the first day and was introduced to the children. Over time the children's contacts with the director increased, and they developed a better notion of both her and then the new director's position and power.

In discussing the children's adaptation to first grade, we first examine the importance of order, control, and rules. We then consider the children's participation in classroom and educational activities.

ORDER, CONTROL, AND RULES

The kids brought certain expectations about "work" to the first grade as a result of their experiences in priming events in preschool. During the first weeks of school they frequently asked about *i compiti* (homework), as they saw that the initial activities were very similar to those of the preschool rather than the more work-related experiences they had anticipated. In fact, the children received no real homework assignments during the initial weeks of the first grade, even though they asked about it almost daily. During the first week, one of the teachers, Arianna, jokingly remarked to Bill that the children kept asking about *i compiti, i compiti*, as if that was all there was to the first grade.

The children also expected that they would not play as much in the first grade as in preschool, and they would have to work more quietly at their desks. Although in the preschool, order sometimes was needed and there were some rules, in first grade the need for order and control was greater and there were more rules. This need for more rules arose, the children believed, because structured educational activities in the first grade demanded a certain amount of order; thus there was less time for play.

The children were very aware of these new rules in preschool as we found out in an interview with Sofia and her mother in the last weeks of the first term of first grade. Sofia, in fact, produced a detailed list of the rules.

Mother: Do you know the rules? What are the rules in first grade?
Sofia: You cannot run in the corridors, you cannot hurt anyone, you have to raise your hand before talking, you cannot lose toys.
Interviewer: You know all the rules!
Sofia: Then you cannot walk around, you cannot shout in the bathroom.

Interviewer: You know everything.
Mother: And then? Perhaps you must wait for your turn.
Sofia: And then, then you have to be silent, write the date. That's all!

In relation to rules, Ball (1980) has argued that initial teacher-child en-counters in classrooms are marked by a "process of establishment," in which exploratory interactions occur or the limits of rules are tested. This process of establishment then brings about a more or less permanent and predict-able pattern of relationships and interactions. Overall we found a similar pattern in children exploring and testing the limits of their new teachers re-garding social order and rules. To smooth the children's adjustment to the new structure of interaction and relationships, the teachers tolerated a good bit of disorder (talking and moving around the room) in the first three weeks of school. From Bill's experience in American first-grade classrooms, the first-grade classes at Giacomo Puccini bordered on the chaotic during these ini-tial weeks. However, the teachers were very calm; after all, they would have these children for 5 years. They gradually introduced more rules and enforced them somewhat more strictly over time.

It is important to note that a certain amount of disorder and confusion was tolerated even after the first month of school, but the limits of this tol-eration were clearly marked. As in the preschool the teachers were clearly in charge. They did not hesitate to raise their voices when the children went beyond the limits: Often they used the phrase *"Adesso basta!"* (Now that's enough!") or warned the children that they were getting angry with them. In addition, many rule violations, failures to stay with the task, and tardi-ness in completing required work were corrected indirectly with humor and teasing as in the preschool. On one occasion, for example, the teacher, Arianna, called on Mario to respond and Luisa shouted out an answer. Arianna turned to Luisa and demanded *"Sei Mario?"* ("Are you Mario?"). All of the children, including Luisa, laughed at this question. On many occa-sions, when a child was talking instead of concentrating on the work, the teachers called out the child's name and then added *"chiacchieronela"* ("big talker"). In another instance one girl, Giuliana, was taking a long time to finish an assignment. Bill was sitting next to her and saw that she was play-ing with her eraser more than writing. The math teacher came by and told her to get to work. When he returned a second time, she had still not made any progress, and the teacher said, "When are you planning to finish? The day after tomorrow?" All the children laughed, and Giuliana smiled at the teacher and got to work.

A final important aspect of the children's adjustment to the new rules and structure of the first grade was their discovery that indeed there was some time for play. The children entered school expecting outside play or recess before and after lunch. After several days in school, however, they had a clearer knowledge of the temporal aspects of the division of work and play. The children discovered that this division was differentiated into time periods more strictly than in preschool. For example, different parts of the school day were signaled by ringing bells, which marked the beginning of class, the time for break and snack (*merenda*) at midmorning, the end the morning class period (and the beginning of lunch), and the end of the school day in the afternoon.

The children were very excited and appreciative of the break for snack at midmorning. After just a few days at school, they cheered and chanted, "*Merenda! Merenda! Merenda!*" when the bell sounded. Then they quickly got out their snacks which varied from store-bought treats to large home-made ham sandwiches. The kids soon created routines during snack time, in which they shared and traded snacks (see Mishler, 1979). Bill, who made sure to bring his own snack, was always included in this sharing and trading. Also the children learned that they could go to visit friends in the other first-grade classrooms.

More important, in the first few weeks older siblings or cousins came to visit the first-grade rooms during snack time. Here we see work in completion of the bridge in priming events as siblings or relatives who told the children about elementary school now went further to check on and see how the younger children were doing in first grade. They often put their arms around their shoulders or took them in their laps, and asked them about their school work and new friends. Thus in the first few weeks of elementary school, the children not only adjusted to the new structural demands but also seized opportunities to use aspects of the new structure to construct and share routines in the new peer culture.

CLASSROOM AND EDUCATIONAL ACTIVITIES

In the first weeks of school the children were introduced to several types of structured educational tasks: literacy activities involving reading and writing, beginning mathematics exercises involving the classification of various objects from their physical and social worlds into groups and art projects.

Initial literacy activities included reading and writing words, phrases, and eventually short narratives. The teachers first concentrated on names by creating tasks and games in which the children learned to read and write all their classmates' names. Then the teachers drew the children's attention to the letters in each name; (for example, by asking the children to group together all names beginning and ending with certain letters. These tasks were followed by activities in which the children read and then copied various rhymes or poems from the blackboard or posters. Although specifics of actual lessons varied a bit across the four class groups, the general goal of learning names and phrases was the same.

Literacy activities in all four groups were also embedded in certain routines that the children experienced earlier in preschool. We will discuss two in particular, general morning discussions and integrating art with literacy.

Morning Routines and Discussions

In Chapter 3 we noted the importance of morning meeting times at Giuseppe Verdi preschool, and we also presented an example of a particular meeting. These meetings were characterized by the lively involvement of the children, who were encouraged by the teachers to state and defend their own opinions and points of view. Before meeting time in the preschool, the teachers usually took attendance, which was kept by placing each child's picture with her or his name on a peg board. Also there was a poster for each month with a place to describe the weather for each day. In describing the weather, the teachers would ask the children what they thought it was, for example, sunny, cloudy, rainy, and so on. When it was decided, one child placed a symbol on the poster.

In first grade these routines concerning attendance and the weather continued in all four classes. However, now the children performed the task with little or no help from the teacher. One child was designated each day to take attendance and to make the appropriate marks (present or absent) on a large attendance sheet on the wall. Another child would fill in the weather on a calendar by drawing a picture in the appropriate place to represent the conditions for that day. The designated child stated her or his opinion before making the drawing, which was usually accepted but at times debated with the other children before a final decision was reached.

As was the case in the preschool, there was also a morning discussion in each of the four classes. The topics of the discussions varied and often were initiated by one of the teachers asking a child about his or her opinion about something. It could be a topic related to their new experiences at school or something about their families or friends. As the weeks progressed, these discussions became more tailored to literacy exercises and reading and writing. The following example of a discussion we videotaped in Prima A about "The Small Shop of Words" occurred in early December 1996 and captures many elements of the teachers' use of a sort of Socratic method in discussion to advance literacy.

The teacher, Arianna, is talking with the children who are seated at their desks with paper and pencils as she walks among them in the room.

"Today we will do a shop of children's words," says Arianna. "A shop of words where children must write only the words they want to write because sometimes adults want the children to write strange things that they do not like. But in this shop where children can write all the words they want, there are no adults that will tell them 'write this word,' 'write this letter.' Children will write their own words. But careful now you have to think."

"With the head," says Rita.

"With the head," responds the Arianna. "Put your hands over your head and think."

"Have you already been thinking Mario?" Arianna asks Mario as he begins to speak. "Wait for some more minutes and reflect because it is very important to think what we like."

Now several children say they are ready. Alfredo says something off topic.

"Careful, Alfredo," cautions Arianna, "we are not talking about the supermarket, we are talking about a shop where children can write the words they like. Mario wanted to talk. Now he can talk. Do you want to tell me a word that children like? Have you already thought about it?"

"Shell, games—,"says Mario.

"Butterflies," interrupts Alfredo.

"Children, let's respect who is talking," says Arianna. "So Mario likes those words. Now I would like to listen to Michela who raised her hand."

"Games," says Michela.

"Then, what else?" says Arianna. "Let's listen to Marta. What words do you like?"

Marta replies, "Games. Cartoons."

Someone says, "Book."

"Let's listen to Viviana," says Arianna.

"But the children know how to write the easy words and that's why they like the easy words," Viviana explains.

"Maybe," says Arianna, somewhat agreeing.

Carla says, "Pencils."

"Why do you like that word?" asks Arianna.

"Because they color very well," Carla responds.

"Are you sure that you really like this word?" asks Arianna. "Let's listen to other children. Fabrizio."

"Games, Lego," says Fabrizio.

"Now we can listen," announces Arianna.

Alfredo says something that is inaudible.

"Alfredo, you don't respect the rules," Arianna says in a gentle voice.

"Lego. Barbie," says Carla.

"I like the bell," offers Marina.

"This is a word that is a bit different," notes Arianna. "Why do you like the word *bell*?

"Because it rings," says Marina.

"I would like to hear also Alberto," says Arianna as she walks over to where Alberto is seated.

"I have nothing in mind," says Alberto.

"Is there anyone who wants to talk?" asks Arianna as she continues pacing the room. "Alfredo, now it is your turn."

"Emilio [the name of a toy robot popular at the time] that you can control with a remote. I also like Lego," says Alfredo.

"And you, Massimo?" asks Arianna stopping near his desk.

But Massimo shakes his head and does not respond.

"Is it possible that you don't like any words?" Arianna asks Massimo. "Do you have anything in mind? OK, you will tell me later."

"I like paintbrushes and Barbie," volunteers Rita.

"Careful, children," says Arianna, "I already told you that, because as words that you like, you are telling me—"

"Toys," says Viviana, finishing the teacher's sentence.

"That's true, the toys that you like. So the words that you like—"

"Also the bell," says Marina.

"The bell is something different, but you're answering with words that are toys, which can be OK," explains Arianna, "but is it clear—the difference between words that you like and toys that you like?"

"I like bicycling," says Michela.

"But it is another thing I am asking you to do," responds Arianna.

"The easiest words with letters we know," says Viviana, "we like it because it is easy."

"Listen, children," says Arianna, "Viviana is expressing her own opinion. She says that the words that children like are the easiest. Do you agree with this? Think about it. Reflect. Put your hands on your head. Is it true that the words the children like the most are the easiest?"

Now the teacher and children hold their hands to their heads and reflect for a few minutes.

"For some children yes, for some others no," says Alberto.

"This is an answer that seems interesting," says Arianna, "but I don't know if your classmates understood. Stand up and try to explain it again."

Alberto stands up at his desk and says, "Because there are children that are able to reflect, and others that are not able."

"But I didn't ask you to look at the difficulties of the words because in this I can help you," says Arianna. "I ask you to say the words that you really like. Fabrizio?"

"The soccer ball because it is beautiful," answers Fabrizio.

"You are confused," says Arianna, "because the problem is, I would like to know which words children like. Mario?"

"I want to write calendar," says Mario.

"Now listen children," implores Arianna. "This conversation remains open because you reflect on this. Today we will start to write words for our shop. Each of you will try to write a word in the way you want, big or small. Now you can think of a word, and I will come and help you write it."

Now the children begin to think, and some to write, as Arianna circulates among them to see what words they decide on.

This discussion is in many ways like the discussion of the human body that occurred in the preschool (see Chapter 3). They are similar in that both teachers encourage all children to participate, and probe the children to express their own points of view and relate the discussion to their experiences and knowledge as children and not simply to answer adult questions. In both cases we see that the children actively participate and offer some innovative responses. It is clear that the morning discussions in the preschool served as priming events in that the children were comfortable with the participant structure in this educational activity and they were used to the probing questions of the teachers to try to get them to think about a number of different possible responses.

However, the two discussions differ in some respects. First, in this discussion in first grade the children sit at their desks and are prepared for a literacy task (printing some of the words for the little shop of words). There is no getting up from their seats and going up to the teacher, and there are fewer interruptions and off-topic talk compared to the example from preschool. It is clear that the children have adopted to the stricter demand for order in first grade. We also see that the teacher reminds them when they speak out of turn or interrupt others.

Second, the teacher, Arianna, uses a style that is somewhat purposely ambiguous. She starts out by stressing that they will make a shop of *children's* words and contrasts this with lessons where children are told what to write by adults. The children are, of course, familiar with the latter because most of the lessons have been of this type, that is, adult-directed for the most part. However, Arianna seems to want to generate a diverse list of words that children like. Therefore, she accepts obvious ones, like the names of toys, and even says that is OK, but she urges them to think of other different words. She also picks up on one contribution that is different, the word *bell*, because it has no obvious link to a toy or game. She also draws attention to Viviana's suggestion that children like the easier words that they know how to spell and write. She asks the children first to think about this "opinion" of Viviana. Later she suggests that they need not worry if the words are big or small because she can help them. The implication is that the shop should be full of a variety of words that the children select. On the other hand, even though the children do the selecting, Arianna constantly probes and pushes them to "think bigger," so to speak, and move beyond the more obvious ones to other words they may like. In the end, she says that the conversation remains open as the children begin to write down or print words for the shop.

As we noted earlier, the teacher's method is somewhat ambiguous in that it appears to us and most likely to the children that there do not seem to be actual words that Arianna has in mind. She does not seem to be sure how she wants the children to respond, only that she wants them to participate, to think, and to come up with words they want. Here we see Italian *discussione* with somewhat of an edge—everyone has the right to participate and all relevant contributions are ratified, but there is a constant probing for more.

Integrating Art into Literacy

In addition to the literacy tasks and discussions described above, the teachers in all four classes used a standard work book for teaching children to read and write. In the workbook there was an exercise where stock phrases were used, such as, "He who looks for _____, will find_____." The children printed out the phrases on their papers than added words to fill the blanks.

At first the teachers accepted almost any words the children used to fill in the blanks as they completed a sentence, but often praised the children's longer and more difficult words. We should add here that in Italian almost all words can be sounded out phonetically so children can easily learn to read and write together. It also means there are few spelling errors and no need to teach spelling as a separate subject as with English in the United States.

After just a few days in using the workbooks, the teachers suggested that the children add words that rhymed in Italian. Now the task was altered a bit as the semantics of the phrases the children came up with were less important than the creativity in rhyming. So for example the children worked with the word "*un elefante*" (an elephant) in the first part of the phrase and then added things like "*un orsetto viaggiante*" (a traveling bear) in the second. Many of the children's productions on this task were highly inventive as shown in Figure 6.1, a creation that the teachers and students in Prima C produced for Bill as a farewell gift when he finished his first round of observations in December 1996. For this gift, the teachers reproduced the stock phrases and then filled in a selection of the children's productions that were copied from the children's worksheets and workbooks. The children then drew pictures to embellish the gift, which were also similar to pictures they drew in their workbooks.

Note in Figure 6.1 that the children produced creative phrases that were related to events in their peer culture (like the loose or dangling tooth) or

Figure 6.1. Literacy and Art in First Grade.

Chi cerca un elefante

trova

un orsetto viaggiante

un dinosauro molto grande

una stella brillante

un lago scintillante

un dente dondolante

un vino frizzante

una luna calante

things that were attractive to them (a giant dinosaur) or whimsical (a traveling bear). We also see the children's impressive artwork, which was a major feature of their literacy productions in first grade. But now it is literacy (reading and writing) that is in the foreground while the artwork is more decorative and in the background as compared to projects in preschool. Thus we see how the first-grade teachers build upon the priming in preschool to develop further the children's literacy skills. It is interesting that the teachers still encourage, and the children very much enjoy, communicating visually through artwork as well as the printed word.

During the second month of first grade the challenge of the literacy activities was extended as the teachers often read a short story to the children, showing pictures from the story as they moved through the narrative. Later the teachers asked the children to draw a scene from the story and then print a description of what was happening in the scene. All these activities presented reading and writing as a means of communication about the world and the children's place in it. The teachers build upon and expand the priming that was begun in preschool as the children's actual level of development in Vygotsky's (1978) terms is extended in that they can now read and write on their own. Yet a new level of proximal development is established as the teachers work with the children on more challenging literacy projects and discussions.

CONCLUSION

Overall, these examples of literacy activities that we earlier discussed in the preschool and here in first grade capture the subtle power of priming events as building a bridge in line with our earlier metaphor in the children's transition from one educational institution to another. Reading and writing in the *Wizard of Oz* project were embedded in the preschool children's more frequent activities of reading and discussing stories with the teachers and the children's depiction of the story in artwork. Once in first grade, the children are involved in more structured lessons, but these lessons also contain aspects of earlier practices in the preschool (most especially discussions and artwork) to embellish their new skills. Thus priming continues as some aspects of earlier preschool experience are progressively deemphasized but are still present. In this way priming insures a smooth and gradual transition as compared to an abrupt disjunction, which could bring about stress and tension in the attempt to learn new skills or even a dislike of schooling itself.

Although the first few weeks of school generally went smoothly, there were some bumps in the road. The children sometimes longed for more playtime when called in from recess, and struggled to remain quietly on task during some literacy assignments. Our observations here were in line with some of the children's own reflections in interviews that we will discuss in Chapter 8. Surprisingly three of the children who experienced the most trouble adjusting to the first grade had been the most active leaders in preschool. At first these three children (Marina, Elisa, and Luciano) had some difficulty when the teachers were not quick to call on them or seemed less appreciative of their answers or ideas than their preschool teachers had been. Except in the case of Luciano, these problems were overcome quickly. And in Luciano's case, the situation improved considerably by December; the teacher, Renata, worked with Luciano and his parents to help him overcome his tendency to act out when he did not receive the special attention he had grown to expect in preschool. By fifth grade, the situation with Luciano had reversed itself completely when Renata saw him as a mature and model student and predicted he would have a smooth transition to middle school.

CHAPTER 7

New Routines, New Friends, and a New Group Identity: The Peer Culture in First Grade

As Bill made his way to Prima A on the first day of class, he saw many parents and children from *Giuseppe Verdi* preschool. All were excited and nervous about this new phase in their lives. In the Prima A classroom the parents of one boy, Alfredo, were especially reluctant to leave their son, so eventually the teachers gently ushered them out. Then the main teacher, Arianna, told us that Alfredo was from Puglia in southern Italy and that he was a little sad about leaving his home. When Arianna asked why he was sad, Stefania from Giuseppe Verdi said, "He misses his grandparents." Some others said he missed his friends; several children (including Marina and Viviana from Giuseppe Verdi) said they would be Alfredo's friends.

So began the first day of elementary school. Everyone was nervous about seeing old friends and making new ones. We discovered that Alfredo's transition was much more challenging than ours because he had left all his friends behind, he was starting completely on his own. Our research on the children's transition, like the task facing Alfredo, was also much larger than it had been at Giuseppe Verdi. We now would be tracking peer relations and peer culture in four different groups with 75 children, compared with the 21 in Giuseppe Verdi.

As the children adjusted to their new teachers and the lessons, routines, and rules of first grade, they also went about constructing a peer culture. There was a local peer culture in each of the first-grade classes and a more general peer culture of first graders. The more general peer culture was affected by environmental factors and relations among the teachers that encouraged interaction and projects between classrooms. Prima A and Prima B were located next to each other on the first floor of the school; Prima C and Prima D were next-door neighbors on the second floor, just above the other first-grade classrooms. The teachers in neighboring classrooms often worked together on joint projects, bringing together Classes A and B, and Classes C and D, for functions in large nearby activity rooms and for joint field trips. In addition, these pairs of classes also frequently used the same outdoor play areas for recess during first grade, and the children were allowed to mingle at break time.

The local and more general peer cultures can be captured in the children's activities and routines, their resistance to adult rules and authority, and their friendships.

CHILDREN'S ACTIVITIES AND GENDER SEPARATION

Gender separation in the first-grade classrooms was noticeably stronger than in preschool. Overall in the first grade, 68.7 percent of the interactive episodes of children's free play were same-gender, as compared with 48.6 percent in the preschool. This difference cannot be explained as a result of gender makeup; the elementary school classes differed little from the preschool in this regard. Also the gender makeup of specific classes was very similar to the overall gender makeup of the first grade and of the preschool. The degree of gender stratification varied across the four first-grade classes. In Prima A, 50 percent of the play episodes were same-gender, very similar to that of the preschool and in line with the highly integrative quality of this group, which we discuss further below. The proportions of same-gender play episodes were much higher for the other three classes: 77 percent in Prima B, 77 percent in Prima C, and 83.3 percent in Prima D. When the different classes played together at recess, 68.7 percent of the episodes recorded in field notes were same-gender during first grade.

What caused these increases in gender separation from preschool to elementary school in the peer culture? One factor was the separation of the children into four classes in first grade with two adjacent classrooms on each of two different floors of the school. As a result, some of the cross-gender friendships established in preschool withered away as there was little opportunity for contact and interaction among these children.

A second factor was the clear bifurcation of the school and the peer cultures, as well as the more limited time for free play in first grade than in preschool. In first grade, free-play time was marked off clearly from school or work time. The children soon realized that their playtime was brief compared to preschool and they had to make the most of it. Snack time or *merenda* initially was a leisurely shared activity. Neighboring children (boys and girls, because desk arrangements usually were mixed-gender) compared and traded snacks, laughed and joked, and sometimes talked about their lessons. Yet when the children realized that, during *merenda*, they could play with school materials or toys they had brought from home, many (especially boys) rushed through the snack to play with superhero figures, handheld games, and other toys. A few boys wadded up paper to use as makeshift balls and organized indoor soccer and basketball games, to gain a head start on popular recess activities. Some girls also finished quickly to play with pocket-sized dolls and other toys, but many were content to talk and joke; sometimes they sang and danced as well. Thus once the children began to exploit some of the limited snack time for free-choice play, we see a shift from gender-integrated play that was the case during *merenda* in the first several weeks of school to primarily same-gender play.

In his field notes Bill observed that the outdoor recess activities during the first several weeks were mostly physical and undirected, mainly running around and climbing on playground equipment. Almost all the boys engaged in this type of play, as did many girls. Other girls and a few boys spent time talking, writing in secret notebooks, or organizing role play. The play yard contained no actual soccer field with goals, but soccer balls were provided.

Over time, the outdoor play became more highly organized into soccer and volleyball games for boys and a few girls; natural features of the play yard such as trees and fences served as goals in soccer. In playing volleyball, the kids usually stood in a circle and took turns batting the ball in the air, trying to keep it from falling to the ground. This activity was more gender integrated than soccer with a few more girls playing than boys. Other games such as La Strega (The Witch, a type of approach-avoidance game; see Corsaro, 2005) were organized primarily by girls, with a few boys participating at times. Also during this time, Bill observed more highly organized run-and-chase games in which boys were aggressors. These latter games set boundaries around the developing gender-segregated groups (Thorne, 1993). Because of the boundary-setting quality of these games, we (like Thorne) did not view them as mixed-gender play. They contributed to a certain degree of gender stratification, however, in that a small group of boys occasionally interfered with and disrupted girls' play. There was one exception to this pattern, however, in that a small group of girls led by one girl, Sandra (who had attended Giuseppe Verdi) often turned the tables on boys and chased them back. This group of girls also at times teased boys and interfered in their soccer games and other play.

In interviews, both the teachers and parents noted the gender separation with some discomfort. They attributed much of it to choice of play and to the boys' more aggressive styles of play. Several of the girls we interviewed in December 1996 (Sonia, Stefania, Irene, and Sofia) said that the boys were too rough and cared only for sports. Elisa, on the other hand, reported that as she began to play a wider variety of games at recess, she played more often with boys. In fact, Renato stated that he played such games with Elisa, and he named her as a friend along with two other girls. Luciano who had often played with girls in preschool made no judgments about girls in the interview; instead he stressed the physical types of play he liked to engage in with boys in his class. These responses in interviews were supported by observations in field notes.

Here we see that shared interests are important in gender separation, as suggested by some researchers (Fagot, 1994; Maccoby, 1999; Maccoby & Jacklin, 1987). These theorists often argue that such interests are precipitating causes that begin in the preschool years. In this case, however, shared interests did not lead to such radical gender separation in the preschool as we saw earlier in Chapter 4. Also some children, such as Elisa, even noted an increase of shared interest with the opposite gender in first grade. As Thorne (1993) argues, it may be more fruitful to directly study gender separation and integration as ongoing processes in situated contexts. As we will discuss in the next chapter, gender relations began to change dramatically in third grade and the children's activities were highly gender integrated by fifth grade. The complexity of these gender-related processes in the peer culture are best captured by longitudinal ethnographies of the type we employ here.

THE UNDERLIFE OF FIRST GRADE

In our many years of ethnographic research of children's peer cultures in preschools in the United States and Italy, we have found that children attempt to evade adult rules through collaboratively produced secondary adjustments, which enable the children to gain a certain amount of control over their lives in these settings (Corsaro, 1985, 2003, 2005). According to Goffman, secondary adjustments are "any habitual arrangement by which a member of an organization employs unauthorized means, or obtains unauthorized ends, or both, thus getting around the organization's assumptions as to what he should do and get and hence what he should be" (1961, p. 189).

Over the course of the year during our observations from September until December and again in May and June, 1997, we found that the children created and participated in a number of secondary adjustments that lead to what can be seen as an "underlife" in the first grade (Goffman, 1961). An *underlife* is a set of behaviors or activities that contradict, challenge, or violate the official norms or rules of a social institution. The underlife of the first grade existed alongside of, and in reaction to, those organization rules that impinged upon the autonomy of the children. In this sense the underlife is an essential part of the children's group identity.

Increasing Movement

The underlife is most apparent in secondary adjustments carried out through the active cooperation of several children. The first thing the children had to get used to in first grade was the rule that they were to stay seated at their desks most of the time during lessons. This restriction of movement was probably one of the biggest differences between the children's everyday activities in first grade as compared to preschool. The teachers were aware that the rule would take some adjustment; therefore, they allowed the children some latitude in leaving their desks especially to consult with other children who were sitting near them. The children, however, devised other strategies to enable more movement around the room and to take breaks from assigned work.

One strategy involved the heavy use of regular and colored pencils in first grade. In preschool the children mainly drew with color markers and rarely used pencils until the end of the last year when they did some exercises in notebooks and other literacy projects. In first grade the children did have the opportunity to draw pictures, but mainly with color pencils and not color markers which were only used for special art projects.

If pencils are used a lot, they need to be sharpened; and a staple in every child's school supply pouch was a small metal sharpener. The children were told by the teachers that when sharpening their pencils they should avoid allowing the shavings to fall on the floor and creating a mess. There were two options: The children could catch the shavings on a piece of paper or some other container and take them to the wastebasket, or they could just go and sharpen their pencils over the wastebasket. Before long the children learned that either of these two methods, but especially the latter, provided them a legitimate reason for leaving their desks and moving around the room.

By the third week the children were busily sharpening their pencils a lot— they set very high standards for how sharp a point was necessary to do their work correctly and neatly! As a result there were lots of trips to the wastebasket in the front of the room and always a lot of stops to talk to, tease, or consult with other kids on the way back to their seats. At times this got so out of hand that a teacher would shout out, "*Troppa confusione!*" ("Too much confusion!") and order the children back to their seats. The kids would usually smile and laugh, and one or two would say, "But we must sharpen our pencils to work." The teachers would agree but demand that things be done in an orderly manner and that the children return immediately to their seats. This command was followed diligently for a while, perhaps even a whole morning or afternoon, but the kids would be back to their old tricks the next day.

Another way to get some autonomy would be to ask to go to the bathroom during work time. Children had opportunities to use the bathroom at break time, before and after recess, and before and after lunch. Normally permission was not granted at other times unless a child had completed her or his work. The children soon realized that if they did complete their work, they could ask to be excused to go to the bathroom, and the teacher would agree. Several times Bill followed a child out into the hallway after the child got permission. In most cases the child went directly to the bathroom, but dawdled on the way back looking into the open doors of other classrooms and waving at other kids and also inspecting various paintings, posters, and other displays on the walls. Some kids stopped and took small toys or candy from the pockets of their coats that were hung in the hallway. They smiled at Bill as they played briefly with the toy or ate the candy, knowing he would not tell on them. In one instance a boy, Renato, had an extra piece of candy, and he gave it to Bill, and they both laughed as they ate this forbidden sweet before returning to the room.

Mimicking the Teachers

Another thing the kids liked to do was to mimic the teachers during break time. Often the teachers would leave the room to tend to business, like making copies, checking on supplies, or getting a coffee. It was expected that the children would be playing during break time and be a bit louder, but not get totally out of control. After the first month a favorite activity would be for one of the children to run to the front of the room, print a word on the board, and then mimic the teacher in making commands to write down the word. This child, usually a girl, would get the others to play along and then inspect their work and almost always point out that their work was sloppy and they could do much better. The one in charge would also demand that other children march to the front of the room and print a certain word on the board. In almost every case this child would make an error on purpose, drawing a reprimand from the teacher about not paying attention and fooling around. They loved to use favorite phrases of certain teachers like "Children calm yourselves!" "But what are you doing?" "Close your mouths!" "Too much talking, little working!" and the often heard *Mamma mia!*

The teacher would often return to the room while these parodies were still in progress, and the kids would scramble to erase the board and return to their seats. The teachers, however, knew what was going on and smiled, letting the children have their fun.

Using Color Markers

One more secondary adjustment is interesting because it captures again how children struggle in making the adjustment from preschool to elementary school. This aspect of the underlife has to do with strategies to get around the restriction on using color markers. Color pencils were to be used in almost all drawings in workbooks because the color markers would bleed through the pages. The children now and then had the opportunity to work with the markers on special drawings in which drawing paper was provided. However, compared to preschool, such opportunities were very rare, and the children's unhappiness with this situation was often a topic of discussion between them.

The children got around this restriction in two ways. First, they often asked to print or draw something in Bill's notebook. Seeing that Bill's notebook was different from their workbooks (after all, Bill was not a real student), they almost always used their color markers in these instances. This example nicely illustrates how the researcher was co-opted by the children and brought into the underlife. At the same time, the first-grade children were printing and drawing things of interest to them, as the preschool children did, and therefore were supplying Bill with data about their literacy skills and peer culture (Corsaro & Nelson, 2003).

A second strategy was to smuggle in something upon which they could draw a picture with their markers without the teacher noticing. A favorite "make-do" (Goffman, 1961) in this instance was Kleenex or napkins they brought with their snacks. One day in Prima A, a girl, Carla, had finished her work. The teacher inspected it and said she did a good job. She was told she could now read from a book of her choice. But as soon as the teacher moved away she took out a Kleenex and began drawing a house with a multicolored rainbow in the background. This choice allowed her to use almost every color marker she had. She glanced up at Bill and cupped her hand shielding the Kleenex and said, "*Guarda*, Bill." ("Look, Bill"). Bill praised her beautiful drawing. Then the teacher approached, and she quickly moved the Kleenex under her desk, only to bring it back out and work on it some more when the teacher moved away. I am sure that the teachers noticed these secondary adjustments, but ignored them as they seldom caused a problem. However, the existence of the shared underlife of first grade was very important to the children. The various secondary adjustments making up the underlife gave the kids a strong sense of autonomy and group identity in this new school, which to their minds had many rules and restrictions.

KEEPING AND MAKING FRIENDS

In considering friendship processes, we look first at Prima A and Prima B. Five children from the preschool group were in Prima A (Marina, Viviana, Stefania, Mario, and Michela). Viviana and Stefania had very similar patterns of peer play: They often played with each other and with Marina, and sought out other friends (all girls) from the preschool in Prima B at break time and recess. Thus they maintained the previous pattern from preschool of playing with several other girls. The two girls also made some new friends among the other girls in their class and managed to find and occasionally play with some old girlfriends from preschool in Prima C and Prima D at recess.

In preschool Mario had most frequently played with Angelo who was now attending first grade in another school. In the first few weeks he initially sought out Renato (in Prima B) and Valerio (in Prima D) at recess, but soon turned to other boys in Prima A and concentrated his play around several of these new friends. Eventually, however, he played with Prima A classmate Marina (one of his first regular female play partners in preschool and first grade).

Michela's play pattern in first grade was similar to Mario's, but progressed differently. Michela had developed a close relationship with Elisa in preschool, and she tried to maintain that relationship: Elisa was now in Prima B and Michela could see her regularly at break time and recess. In the first weeks, Michela often sought out Elisa and they played comfortably as they had in preschool. After that time, however, Elisa began playing more with others, leaving Michela with other playmates or even alone. The separation was gradual: Elisa and Michela continued to play together, but Michela now also sought out new friends. She primarily played with other girls in Prima A who were not from her preschool class.

In the preschool, Marina had played regularly with a wide number of friends including two boys (Luciano and Renato). She maintained this pattern in first grade, playing regularly with former friends from preschool (Elisa, Federica, Renato, and Sonia in Prima B; and Sofia, and Viviana in Prima A). She also sought out and continued to maintain her friendship with Luciano (in Prima C). In addition, Marina made several new friends in Prima A, including a boy, Mario, whom she had rarely played with when they were in preschool.

Four children from Giuseppe Verdi were in Prima B (Elisa, Renato, Federica, and Sonia). We have already discussed Elisa's changing relationship with Michela (in Prima A). As she gradually played less with Michela, Elisa maintained close friendships with Federica, Sonia, and Renato in her class and Marina, Sofia, and Viviana in Prima A. She made several new friends both boys and girls, in Prima B.

Renato found himself in a somewhat difficult situation because there were no other boys from his preschool class in Prima B. Like Mario who was in the same situation in Prima A, Renato made friendship bids to other boys in his new class, but they were rejected. The other boys had been together in their former preschool and strongly resisted new friends. Therefore, Renato played primarily with former friends from preschool in Prima A and Prima B (Elisa and Federica in Prima B; Sofia, Marina, and Mario in Prima A) as well as Luciano, who was in Prima C.

The other two children in Prima B (Federica and Sonia) had very similar patterns of peer relations. Both confined their play primarily to each other and other girls: Elisa in Prima B and Marina and Sofia in Prima A from the preschool class and two new girls from Prima B. Our field notes also showed a pattern in which Sonia became more and more deeply involved in an exclusive clique in Prima B, which centered around one of her new friends, Stella.

Prima C included only three children from the preschool (Luciano, Michele, and Stefania). Michele, the mildly autistic boy, did very well in first grade: he accomodated to the need to stay at his desk, and he became more spontaneous and more reflective in literacy activities and lessons. For example, when Bill returned to the elementary school in May 1996, Michele was the first to greet him and took him around to show and tell him about several school projects as well to show Bill his own work and talk about it. Bill looked over at the teacher, Renata, who was smiling approvingly. No words were needed to capture this strong improvement in Michele's social and cognitive skills. On the other hand, Michele's participation in the peer culture still remained primarily peripheral. He often ran around alone on the playground and did not develop any close friendships. However, he was considered an active member of his class, and the other children never teased or mocked him.

Luciano, finding himself the only boy from the preschool outside of Michele in Prima C, quickly made friendship bids to the other boys in his class. He and one of the these boys, Giuseppe, soon formed a strong dyad that was frequently joined by other boys from Prima C. Luciano thus showed a major change from the preschool, where he played with a wide range of other children including both boys and girls. At times he still played with two friends from preschool: Valerio from Prima D and Renato from Prima B. He also sought out, or was sought out by, Marina from Prima A for play or conversation.

Stefania was the only girl who found herself without a former girlfriend from preschool in her first-grade class. This problem may have contributed to some crying and disputes with Luciano in the first weeks of school. Frequently, however, Stefania sought out former girlfriends from Giuseppe Verdi at recess, especially Carlotta and Irene from Prima D. She also began to play more frequently with other girls in Prima C.

Four children (Carlotta, Irene, Sandra, and Valerio) from the preschool were in Prima D. Carlotta and Irene further strengthened a close friendship that they had formed in the preschool, and continued to play with Sandra in their class and Viviana and Sofia from Prima A. Both of these girls, however, began to concentrate their play on other girls in Prima D. In preschool Sandra had played with a wide range of children, both boys and girls. She was very independent and continued this pattern in first grade: She now played with new girls from Prima C and Prima D, but her most frequent playmates were Carlotta and Irene, her classmates in preschool and also in Prima D.

Valerio showed a pattern similar to Sandra's. In the preschool he played primarily with Angelo, Mario, and Renato, but also regularly with several girls. In first grade he sought out Mario (in Prima A) and Renato (in Prima B) at recess, but now seldom played with girls as he developed friendships with new boys in Prima D.

Overall, when we compare peer relations in the preschool to those in first grade, we see some similarities, some extensions of emerging patterns, and some major divergences (see Corsaro, Molinari, Hadley, & Sugioka, 2003). In many ways the structure of peer relations and friendships in Prima A was most like that of the preschool group. Marina, Sofia, and Viviana continued to play regularly with several of their classmates, and both Michela and Mario moved from more exclusive to more inclusive play patterns. Marina was able to continue a pattern of diverse peer relations that included both boys and girls, mostly in Prima A and Prima B. She even managed to maintain her friendship with Luciano, with whom she had relatively few opportunities for contact. Although the developing friendship structure in Prima D was more exclusive than that of the preschool group, this class contained no strong cliques except for Carlotta and Irene whose best friendship was established in preschool and became more exclusive in first grade.

Prima B and Prima C show the greatest contrast with the preschool. Prima B contained an exclusive group of boys from the start: these new boys separated themselves from girls and resisted the entry of Renato and two other boys. In addition, over the first several months and continuing into second grade, an exclusive clique of girls developed including Sonia and Federica. Although Elisa and Renato did not take active part in such exclusion, Renato may have become more involved in the all-boy group: He was somewhat successful at joining their play in second grade.

Finally, we also saw the development of gender-differentiated friendship relations for Luciano and Stefania in Prima C. Luciano, who had played frequently with girls in preschool, and Stefania, who had occasionally played with boys, engaged almost totally in same-gender play with classmates in Prima C.

CONCLUSION

In this chapter we have portrayed the children's production of and participation in a new peer culture. We described their peer activities and how the four first-grade groups became more gender differentiated as compared to the preschool group we studied. We also noted the development of an underlife of the preschool, which was important for several reasons. By challenging various school rules through a variety of secondary adjustments, the children gained autonomy and developed a strong group identity.

The very creation of the underlife displayed the children's intricate knowledge of their new school in terms of both its structure and rules as well as the expectations, styles, and personalities of the teachers. In this way the peer culture contributes in positive ways to a successful transition. We also noted the complexity and differences in the four groups in how the children went about keeping and making new friends in first grade. Here we saw in two classes some overall similarity in terms of friendship relations to the preschool class we studied. On the other hand, the other two classes were much more differentiated by gender and, to some degree, status when compared to preschool.

CHAPTER 8

Reflections on the Transition to First Grade

In this chapter we present and analyze interviews with parents, children, and elementary school teachers in which they reflect on the children's transition to first grade. We conducted the interviews a few weeks before the end of the first term of first grade, in late November and early December. Here we first consider the teachers' assessments of how the children were adjusting to first grade, and then compare and contrast the teachers' reflections with those of the children and their parents.

Of the two teachers working in each class, we interviewed only the teachers of humanistic subjects (Italian, history, art, and so on) since they would continue teaching in the same class for the 5 years of elementary school and we would be able to interview the same teachers over all 5 years. (The math teachers were employed on a yearly base.) We met the teachers 2 weeks before the school started, presented our research program, and together with them decided that Bill would observe in the school four mornings per week, observing one morning in each class, when the teacher of Italian was present.

The four teachers interviewed were all female, with long experience in teaching. The oldest teacher had been working in elementary schools for almost 30 years, while the youngest for more than 15 years. When we collected the data, they all had been working in Giacomo Puccini elementary school for at least 12 years and therefore had a strong sense of continuity in the same community. They often worked in pairs; that is, children of two classes met and worked together on a regular basis. In particular, Arianna and Letizia (Prima A and B) were one team, while Renata and Giusi (Prima C and D) were the second team. All four classes also participated in common projects organized by the school, like parties or meetings with the parents.

Our first impression of the teachers was very good. They did not seem preoccupied with the observations, but rather appeared very confident about their professional abilities. However, when asked in the first interview how they felt about the presence of Bill as an observer in the classes, they all admitted that they were very conscious of his presence, and that at the beginning they behaved differently because of it. After the first weeks, they felt more confident, especially because they realized how much Bill was able to be "like a child" and "camouflage" himself within the group. They also all agreed that the children immediately accepted Bill and were very proud of his presence in their class.

What was more interesting was that when reflecting on this experience all the teachers said that they felt it acted as a stimulus, a pressure to engage more in their work, as expressed by Letizia:

> I think he allowed me not to work in a different way, but to create richer situations for the whole class because I was conscious that there was an adult person in my class. This stimulated me to arrange more things, to organize my teaching in a better way then I would do if he were not present.

The observations were therefore an opportunity for the teachers to improve the standards of daily teaching, and for this reason they all agreed that they would be happy to repeat the experience.

TEACHERS' APPROACH TO FIRST GRADE

The first interview was mainly centered around the evaluation of their work as teachers in general and their philosophy and approach to teaching first grade in particular. When asked which aspects of their work they liked most, teachers made reference especially to three aspects: First, they enjoy the life with children, characterized by enthusiasm and sincerity, and the possibility of knowing what they really think; second, they felt that children helped them remain young and lively; and third, they appreciated the opportunity to participate in courses about new ways of teaching. What they liked least was the bureaucratic part of teaching, as well as problems with discipline and the necessity to produce evaluations of individual children.

Educational Philosophy

The educational philosophy they followed as teachers centered on both learning and social relations. In respect to learning, teachers stressed that it is important for children to develop an appreciation for learning new things. This does not mean that it is easy to learn, but that every child can make progress in her or his efforts in this direction. For example, Giusi gave this explanation:

> I try to help children understand that learning in school can be a beautiful thing. You can love learning, and this does not imply that you should not make any effort; on the contrary they can understand that they have to work hard, and that they do this because it is beautiful, not because they are obliged to.

When focusing on the importance of social relations, teachers mentioned the values of solidarity and friendship among classmates. They believed that having good relations within the class is an important starting point for learning processes.

Following these general values, the teachers stated that they had two main goals for first grade: helping children learn to read and write, and helping them learn to establish friendship bonds. One teacher, Letizia, emphasized a problem that she was facing with the new class, that was related to both these goals. She was witnessing a rapid change in childhood, linked to the velocity of changes in the society:

> We have new classes every 5 years, and in this period society has changed so much that children are very different. We can easily note this fact: These children are more capable of interacting with different kinds of information. For example, they can draw, listen, do more things at the same time, but they cannot concentrate on one thing. They consume experiences in a very rapid way; they do not try to deepen [their experiences], and also have difficulties in listening.

Although the teachers did not point out all of the other problems that they had to face with these classes in the first months of school, they did mention some difficulties in learning demonstrated by individual children. In all the classes, children showed very different levels in prerequisites for literacy learning: Some children were already able to read and write, while others absolutely were not.

These individual differences among children were one of the main reasons teachers made reference to when stating that they thought that the American school system, based on changes of teachers every year, was not facilitating the two goals mentioned above, that is, learning and developing social relations. All of the teachers were in agreement that in Italy when a school year starts, the teachers do not have to be worried about how many things they have to teach the children, and therefore they can take it easy and plan long-range objectives. Year after year, the class becomes more

homogeneous, and the development of strong bonds among the children and with the teachers are important premises for the whole educational and didactic work of the teachers.

There was one point on which the teachers expressed doubt: Five years is a long period, for children to have reference to only two teachers. The consequence of this may be, for example, a difficult transition to middle school. Another consequence may be difficulty in establishing relationships with different adults. For this reason the teachers expressed favorable opinions about having specialized teachers for some subjects, like second language, gymnastics, and music. One teacher suggested that maybe a period of 2–3 years with the same teacher might be a good "compromise" between the two school systems.

Appreciation of Priming Events

The last question of the first interview was aimed at understanding what teachers considered priming events to be. Answering this question, they raised several points. They agreed about the important preparation made by preschool teachers for children's transition to first grade. They also stated that their first months in school were devoted to maintaining continuity with preschool, based on play, telling stories, singing songs, making rhymes. They only gradually started to work more directly toward the curriculum for first grade, and this, as confirmed by our observations, helped to make the transition very smooth.

One teacher, Renata, made reference to a different priming event, an event useful for future life experiences, that is, visits to museums. Her statements were very interesting since they confirmed the importance of the notion of priming events for educators, whose work is aimed at preparing today's children for life in Western society.

> I think that priming events are some experiences that we have now and that will continue in our life. For example, [when] we went to the museum, . . . [the] children asked, "What is a museum?" It is a place where we go now, but where we will also go when we will be grown up, and this is important.

CHALLENGES AND SUCCESSES
IN INDIVIDUAL TRANSITIONS

As part of the interviews, we asked the teachers to offer us a brief description of each of the eight children whose parents had agreed to be interviewed with their children throughout our study. Their descriptions were mainly centered on how particular children adapted to the school transition in first grade. In discussing these responses, we will compare and contrast them with the reflections of some of the parents and children regarding the transition period.

For some children, the transition was very smooth. They had done very well in preschool, as both the observation and the interviews with preschool teachers confirmed, and they were very active and competent in first grade, right from the beginning.

Some other children also had a smooth transition, but the descriptions offered by the teachers were somewhat inconsistent with the data we had collected in the preschool. Consider Elisa, for example. Elisa had a very close friend in preschool, Michela, who after the transition was assigned to a different class. In preschool these two girls were always together and this limited somewhat their interactions to the other children. Their relationship was the only one close to a clique in the preschool. After the transition, Elisa's teacher, Letizia, described her this way: "A very mature and altruistic girl, she is helping the other children and she is very generous and open to everybody, especially to a girl, Giulia, who needs help."

The interview with Elisa and her parents confirm the teacher's observation that she adapted to changes in peer relations and widened her friendships compared to preschool. Let us consider what Elisa says when interviewed by Bill about friends.

Bill: In school, do you play with your friends from Giuseppe Verdi school?
Mother: During recess.
Elisa: Yes, yes, because they are those that I know better, that I like, I like to play with them.
Bill: Do you still play a lot with Michela?
Elisa: Yes, because my class is very close to her class, so I play with them, with Michela but also Marina and Viviana.

Changes in the peer culture for some children make the transition very challenging but can result in a more positive integration within the new group of classmates.

For other children, the transition was more difficult, and they had somehow to struggle to restore their place within the new peer group. This was true, for example, for Renato who was in a class where the majority of children were girls and where the other boys were already very close because they came from the same preschool. The composition of the classes in terms of gender is an important aspect both for peer culture and for children's transitions.

Renato's teacher confirmed that he initially had a hard time adjusting in first grade because he was not accepted by the few other boys in his class. Her assessment was in line with our interview of Renato and his parents.

Interviewer: Are there other children from preschool in your class?
Renato: There are Elisa, Federica, and Sonia.
Mother: They are girls ... yes, he finds it difficult to enter the group of boys in his class, because the other four boys come from the same preschool. He is trying to join the group. ... They are very close, it is not easy for him to join the group.
Interviewer: Who are your best friends in your class?
Renato: Elisa, Sonia, Federica, Alessandro.
Mother: Alessandro did not attend Giuseppe Verdi.
Interviewer: Do you like Alessandro?
Renato: Uh, not so much, sometimes he makes me laugh.

Mother and child share concerns about the problems Renato encounters to find his place among a group where the only boys are very close and not so open to new friends. He mentions the girls that he knows from preschool as best friends, and also adds one boy, who is actually not so nice, but probably the nicest boy in the class.

Among the children we were following, another child, Luciano, was described by his teacher, Renata, in a way that was surprising to us who saw Luciano as a leader and very active member of the preschool class. The preschool teachers, in fact, described him as a very competent boy, both in the school's activities and with friends, and our observations confirmed that he was very active in the peer culture. Renata, however, described Luciano as one of the children who had not had a very easy transition. When describing him, she noted:

> Luciano is one of the few children [about whom] I did not agree with the preschool teachers' reports. My opinion is that in the transition he has probably lost the role of leader that he played before in preschool because he found other children who were more advanced than he was academically, especially girls in the class. He is hyperactive and his mother confirmed that this has long been the case. This behavior often puts him in conflict with the rules in elementary school. As for his academic progress, I thought he could learn faster than he actually did. He is somewhat of a perfectionist and this characteristic leads him to begin his work over three or four times because he is not satisfied with his work.

Bill's observations in Luciano's classroom confirmed many of the problems Renata noted above. Luciano did seem in almost constant need of attention.

He also had some problems staying at his desk and on task as his mother feared he might in her earlier interview. Luciano, however, in our second interview saw things quite differently than his teacher.

Interviewer: What did you find different from preschool to first grade?
Luciano: That you have to write a lot, read and stay still, make drawings on your notebook, while in preschool we were drawing and playing much more.
Interviewer: That's right, and what do you prefer, preschool or first grade?
Luciano: First grade.
Mother: Really?
Luciano: Yes.
Interviewer: So you like the new things, that is, reading, writing?
Luciano: I used to try reading and writing in preschool, but I could not make it.
Interviewer: Have you learned now?
Luciano: Yes.

Note that Luciano's mother seems surprised when he says he prefers first grade to preschool. What might be the reason for this difference between the teacher's assessment, the mother's expectations, and Luciano's claims? First, Luciano does note that it was a big change to have less time to play and for the need to stay still. Therefore, he was aware of the difficulties. Second, where the teacher sees some problems in learning, Luciano feels he has improved his literacy skills. Here we should point out that while Luciano was a verbal leader in preschool, he was not among the children who could read and write easily when they entered first grade. It seems the first-grade teacher had higher expectations of him based on the reports of the preschool teachers than Luciano had for himself. Finally, although Luciano does not mention his peer relations in first grade, he quickly fit in and made many new friends in his class and among the other classes. Regarding peer relations, Luciano maintained and even expanded his leadership role. This was something the first-grade teacher seemed less aware of as she concentrated on his classroom behavior.

In the interview we carried out at the end of the school year, the teacher confirmed that in her opinion Luciano was a child who still had several difficulties, because he was not confident and constantly needed attention and praise. He was also sometimes aggressive with the other children. As we will see in the next chapter Luciano overcame these problems and was eventually seen by his teacher as a model student.

These descriptions are important because they provide us information on the complexity of transitions in early education and the importance of studying these transitions longitudinally. In general, the children we studied made a smooth transition, but we also were able to identify certain problems of adjustment. One of the reasons for these problems may be due to the fact that some children who had established leadership roles during the 3 years of preschool encountered some difficulties in first grade, because they did not always receive the attention and praise from their teachers and peers to which they had become accustomed. This is why they sometimes acted out to gain attention. After the third month of the term, however, we found that most of these children had overcome their problems. We also discovered in the interviews that certain children who were more quiet, shy, and sensitive in preschool (such as Mario and Valerio) blossomed in first grade and overcame these problems.

TEACHERS' AND PARENTS' REFLECTIONS ON PARENTAL INVOLVEMENT

Both teachers and parents made reference to parental involvement in the life of the school in first grade in the interviews. However, there were clear differences in their assessments. The teachers expressed a positive evaluation related to parental involvement in the school's life, even though they observed huge differences between families actively involved on a regular basis and families that are completely absent from school.

Parents reported problems with new rules in elementary school. They made reference to rules that they were not so happy to accept because they disrupted routines in their involvement in their children's school lives. The problems resulted from the rule that restricted parents' entry into the school and the classrooms after the first week. The parents, who were used to having daily contacts with the teachers and the class in preschool, were now asked to drop off and pick up their children in the courtyard outside the school. The parents' unhappiness seemed to extend beyond the specific rule to a general feeling that the elementary school was less open to parental involvement than the preschool. As Elisa's father points out:

> In the preschool you could always enter the class and you could see their work and projects as they developed, you could participate more, and so on. So now all we can do is to listen to what Elisa tells us about the school and what is happening. Or sometimes we can meet the teacher, but we cannot actually see what Elisa does. I could enter in the first days,

and then the classroom was not so warm or accommodating as the preschool.

As one consequence of this change, the parents experience a greater separation between families and elementary school, which could affect parents' general knowledge of the school. This finding suggests that some of the strong collectivist elements of the preschool system may be difficult to maintain in the elementary school.

CONCLUSION

The four teachers we interviewed agreed that their classes had proceeded very well during the first year. Given the different individual levels observed at the beginning of school, at the end of the year the classes were more homogeneous and the differences in learning abilities were reduced. One teacher noted that in the final period her class had its own identity, evidenced by the good relationships established among the children and with the teachers.

Both children and parents stated that they suffered adjustment problems. The children had to adjust to the new peer culture, and this adjustment varied depending on the different situations of the new class groups, while parents complained that certain elementary school rules limited their entry into their children's classrooms and restricted their involvement in their children's school lives more generally.

CHAPTER 9

Becoming a Community of Learners and Friends: The School and Peer Cultures in Grades 2–5

Intensive observations of the school and peer culture continued on an everyday basis for about half of the first grade year. After that, Bill returned to the school for 6 weeks of observations in May and June of first, second, third, and fifth grade. We also interviewed the teachers and a group of eight children and their parents in the spring of every grade of elementary school and when the children were in the second year of middle school. Finally, Bill kept in touch with each class by sending cards, letters, and e-mail messages during his time away from the school. In return he received hundreds of letters, cards, drawings, and e-mail messages over the course of the 5 years of elementary school and correspondence from some children after they went on to middle school. These materials provide a rich set of data for charting the children's progress through elementary school and their transition to middle school.

One letter was sent from Carlotta to Bill on February 5, 1997, when the children were in the second term of first grade. In her letter Carlotta draws a picture on one side of the page and prints a letter to Bill on the other side. Figure 9.1 shows the picture Carlotta drew. She is dressed in a nurse's costume for Carnevale, and she addresses both Bill and her friends, who are drawn in the background, using the type of talk bubbles found in comic books. To the other children she says, "*Qualcuno vuole una puntura?*" ("Anyone wants a shot?"—Carlotta has made a slight grammatical error). Several of the children in the background respond also via the talk bubbles with one girl saying she is afraid, another crying "help!", and a third girl telling the other two to have a little courage and take their shot. Carlotta says to Bill, "*E tu Bill vuoi una puntura?*" ("And you, Bill, do you want a shot").

On the other side of the paper Carlotta prints a letter to Bill in which she tells him she likes him and describes a field trip the class took to see a puppet show. She then tells Bill she is doing well and that the weather in

Figure 9.1. Carlotta's Drawing for a Letter to Bill.

Italy has been so-so. She goes on to tell Bill what she got for Christmas and that she dressed as a nurse for Carnevale. She ends the letter by telling Bill she misses him and that the teacher told her that he would be coming back to visit the school in the spring.

Another letter sent by Stefania in December 1998, when the children were in third grade, shows a clear movement from relying equally on art and text to communicate to relying primarily on text with art used as embellishment. (For a detailed discussion of Stefania's letter, see Corsaro & Nelson, 2003.) The letter was written entirely in cursive with few grammatical errors. Stefania describes how the children will soon be able to see a movie that is based on a book that they read in class. She is clearly excited by this, and her excitement captures the importance of literacy in the peer culture. Stefania goes on in her letter to ask Bill about Christmas customs in the United States and talks about how Christmas is celebrated in Italy. Here she draws small pictures of a Christmas tree and a type of cake eaten at Christmas in Italy. She also tells Bill about the new English teacher and draws a picture of her. Stefania writes that the teacher has taught them the song "White Christmas," which they sang at a Christmas party. Finally, she tells Bill that new girls have joined the second grade and that they came from Germany, Ghana, and Italy (see Corsaro & Nelson, 2003).

Stefania's letter reveals that children use the literacy activity of writing letters to report relevant and important events. For example, almost all of the letters Bill received when the children were in fourth grade reported that Federica (a girl we first observed in preschool) had moved to another city and was no longer at Giacomo Puccini. In addition, as in all the letters sent to Bill, artwork played an important role in Stefania's letter, showing that the combination of art, reading, and writing, which began in preschool, is still apparent in third grade.

Carlotta's and Stefania's letters provide us a nice introduction to changes and developments in the school and peer culture after Bill completed fulltime participant observation in first grade to the midpoint of third grade. We now turn to additional patterns in developments in the school and peer cultures based on field notes Bill made during periods of participant observation during the second, third, and fifth year of elementary school and from letters, cards, and gifts the children wrote or made for Bill over all 5 years of elementary school.

THE SCHOOL CULTURE

In second and third grade, lessons in Italian and math became more demanding for the children, and in third grade they also began studying

English with a separate teacher. However, certain routines, especially discussion, artwork, and field trips, that were common in preschool and first grade continued to occur, and new educational tasks were often embedded in these routines.

Family History Project

In second grade in Class C the teacher designed a long term project related to family and family history with several elements. The children had a homework assignment in which they were to talk with their grandparents about their specific families (how the grandparents met, when their parents, aunts, and uncles were born, and so on). Later, at a normal meeting time an elderly gentleman visited the class and narrated his life history.

During the time when Bill visited the class in May 1998, each child with help from the teacher, Renata, constructed a family tree (*albero genealogico*) beginning with their grandparents and specifying in descending order to themselves and their brothers and sisters if they had any. Working with the children, Bill constructed his family tree in his own notebook. Many of the children did not have brothers or sisters, and the boy from the largest family in the class had only three siblings. Bill differed a great deal from the children because he had many siblings as did his parents.

In a class discussion near the end of third grade, Renata noted that more than half the class were only children. She asked the children why they thought their families were so small, and she got some interesting responses.

"Children are a lot of work," offered Luciano.

"Yes," responded Stefania, "young children cause parents to lose sleep and get bags under their eyes."

"Children are expensive," said Giovanna. "Parents have to buy clothes, food, and toys."

The discussion continued with many children participating and excitedly raising their hands to get a turn at talk. The topic changed a bit with a discussion of the effects of children on mothers.

"Women do not want to lose their physical shape," said Giorgio and everyone laughed.

"My mother stayed home from work after my little sister was born," noted Stefania.

"My mother went back to work when my brother was 10," added Sergio.

This part of the discussion is interesting as the children display knowledge of the fact not only that children create work for their parents and are expensive, but also that having children affects the mother's work life. One child, Davide, expands this theme by noting that children often worked with parents on farms or in stores in the past. However, this is not typical today.

Davide may have picked up this knowledge from his conversation with grandparents or from the visitor's talk. Renata praised the children for these comments and noted that children were expected to work and help their parents more in the past.

Overall, this family project, including the discussion of reasons for small families, is similar to projects the children participated in earlier in nursery school. In this case, while the participant structure of the activity is very similar to preschool, the children's activities and discussion are more advanced and intellectually sophisticated. In fact, the discussion of low fertility is very similar to adult explanations (including demographers') for this pattern in Italy today (Italy has one of the lowest birth rates in the world). This is especially true regarding the expense of children and parents' desires to be able to help their children have a high quality of life. No doubt the children may have been participants in discussions of this type in the family where debate and discussions are regular and encouraged (Pontecorvo, Fasulo, & Sterponi, 2001). So we see that the classroom activity benefits both from priming in the preschool and the home.

Literacy and Math

In another of the second-grade classes during projects that encouraged literacy development, the children gave oral reports of books they had chosen and read from the library. The presentations were often lengthy and complex, and many children asked questions and made comments on their classmates' reports. In yet another project that followed a trip to a park and a visit to a garden show, the Classes C and D returned to discuss what they saw and drew beautiful pictures to recapture the experience. Thus the children's ability in creating art that began in preschool was still important and useful in capturing experiences in second grade. The children's artistic talents continued to develop, now used to embellish and build on literacy skills.

In second and third grade the children often worked on math assignments that involved not only practice and drilling in computations (addition, subtraction, multiplication, and division), but also word problems that challenged their reading abilities and logic skills. Thus we see that math was often integrated with reading and writing and built on the children's general instruction in literacy. Math was taught by a different teacher from the main teacher in each class, and there was some turnover of math teachers in all four classes. Although having several different math teachers did not seem to have a negative effect on the children's learning, it was something that the parents expressed concern about in interviews. The head teachers also expressed to Bill a concern about the turnover of math teachers, but also noted it was good for the children to have experiences with different teachers for different subjects before they made the transition to middle school where they would have many different teachers.

Studying English

After not being able to visit the school during fourth grade, Bill was able to return for the last 6 weeks of fifth grade which were the children's last weeks in elementary school. He brought a special gift for all the children, which he was able, with help from the English teachers, to incorporate into an English lesson. Bill brought each child a dollar coin that bore a picture of the Native American explorer Sacagawea. He also brought a book detailing Sacagawea's life, most especially her role in the explorations of Lewis and Clark.

In the English classes Bill passed out the coins and described Sacagawea's picture, pointing out that in the picture she was carrying her infant son on her back during the Lewis and Clark expedition. Bill also summarized the story in the book, talking slowly in English. There was a map of the United Sates in the class that Bill made use of during the story, and he only had to clarify certain points here and there in Italian. The children had many questions, which they almost always were able to ask in English with some help from Bill and the teachers.

After the story the children sang several songs in English. For some of the songs the children and teacher had composed new lyrics in English that were quite inventive. Also the children took turns reading from their English workbooks, and again Bill was very impressed with their performance. In fact, these fifth-grade Italian children could read English at a comparable level, in Bill's judgment, to many third-grade American children. However, the Italian children had more difficulty in speaking English well. It appeared to Bill that the English teachers used many of the same instructional methods (involving music and art) that the Italian preschool and Italian teachers had used to teach reading and writing Italian. These techniques worked well. However, a drawback in Italy for children learning to speak English is that they hear the language so infrequently outside of the classroom, as almost all English media for the cinema and television is dubbed into Italian.

Documentation

In all the fifth-grade classes the children's activities related to the new subjects of science and history were displayed in various ways in the classrooms. Many of these posters, maps, and diagrams captured the children's work in striking ways and paralleled the ways that schoolwork was displayed in the preschool. So we see that the same general pattern of planning, doing, and reproducing that is the hallmark of early education in this region of Italy was preserved and expanded in the public elementary school. The projects on the walls of the classrooms and in some public areas of the preschools serve as memory traces of the groups' activities and accomplishment over their 5 years of elementary school. Thus again we see a similarity to and continuation of elements of the early educational philosophy of Reggio Emilia which is so well known outside the country.

Many of the displays went beyond artwork, to maps and diagrams that the children had produced in the computer lab. These productions are notable because the computer lab was introduced into the school during the fourth year of the class we studied. In fact, one of the first things Bill noticed was the lack of computers in the school when he started his observations in the fall of 1996. Now, however, this particular school had caught up fast, and the children seemed very comfortable with the use of computers and many also had access to computers in their homes.

Friendship Gifts

The children's accomplishments over the last 2 years while Bill was away from the school can be captured in two sets of activities. The first involved the planning of a surprise birthday party for Bill by Classes C and D that displayed many of the children's advanced artistic, foreign language, and literacy skills. The second also revolved around Bill's birthday as the children in Classes A and B gave him a collection of poems they had written about war and peace.

At the birthday party the children presented Bill with individual gifts which were highly unique works of art. Many children made various types of pop-up birthday cards with greetings and messages. Others constructed paper houses, boats, or airplanes that contained hidden messages that one found by pulling a string or opening windows, or moving various parts of the constructions. These messages usually conveyed a greeting of happy birthday in English or Italian, but also good-byes and farewells to an adult friend that many of the children realized they may not see again.

In addition to the individual gifts, all the children in Classes C and D wrote messages in a special friendship book entitled "*Per un Amico*" ("For a Friend") that contained poems, memories, and quotes from well-known authors along with blank pages that could be used for a journal or to record appointments. The children filled these pages with messages in English to Bill about the close friendship that had developed with him over the years. Below is a message from Luciano:

THE YEARS GO ON, BUT YOU ARE
NEVER OLD
THE YEARS GO ON AND YOU'LL ALWAYS
BE MY FRIEND

HAPPY BIRTHDAY
Luciano

This message captures the special nature of Bill's relationship to the children as an adult friend. For children, birthdays and aging are very important and obvious aspects of their lives. But unlike a peer, Bill is an adult friend and in this way seems not to age and the friendship seems not to change.

As noted earlier, the children of Classes A and B gave Bill a collection of poems—many of them quite impressive—that they had written about war and peace for history class. The children had discussed World War II and especially the role of the partisans who fought against the Fascists in northern Italy. The partisans not only had been important in ending the war and the rule of the Fascists, but also in representing fraternity and civil society. These aspects are captured in a moving poem (translated from the Italian) produced by Marina from Class A:

For a Happy World

I dreamed that men
One day will wake up
And will easily understand
That they are made to live together
As siblings

I dreamed that men
One day will take their hands
And will understand that they were created
To help and love each other

I dreamed that men
One day will hug as brothers
And will forget without difficulty
That they fought for a long time

I dreamed that men
One day will work to make a better world
And of war will remain only
A bad memory

I dreamed that men
One day will discover the importance
Of peace

I dreamed that men
One day will not need any more
Of prisons and of threats
Because they will become inseparable friends

This morning I dreamed
Fraternity.

This poem (and other work like it) made both the teachers and parents of the children proud and especially satisfied at the children's development and achievements in their 5 years of elementary school. We as researchers also feel proud of the children and privileged to have shared in their lives in their transition from preschool to elementary school and throughout the elementary school years.

THE PEER CULTURE

When Bill returned for observations in May and June of the children's second, third, and final year in elementary school, he saw interesting changes in the children's peer relations and cultures.

Gender Segregation

In the second grade the children's outside play became more routine with mainly gender-segregated physical play (soccer for boys and gymnastics and volleyball for girls). For the girls, the gymnastics involved doing handstands, often against the walls, and turning flips in the grass. Some of the girls were very good at this and reported to Bill that they were taking gymnastics lessons after school. The volleyball play involved standing in a circle and hitting the ball and trying to keep it from falling to the ground. The children would count the number of hits the ball was kept in the air and praise those who kept the ball from touching the ground at the last minute. A few boys played in the volleyball groups which normally had five or six children in each group. The children also invited Bill to play, which he often did.

Bill only occasionally played soccer because the games were fast moving and Bill could not keep up with them by third grade, even though he was physically larger than the children. Many of the boys had become quite good players, and games were more organized than in first grade with some games carrying over from one day to the next. Two or three girls played on a regular basis and displayed skills similar to the boys.

In third grade, girls and boys played a form of *la strega*, which we first documented in the play of kids in preschool. In the elementary school version it was very similar to what is known as freeze tag in the United States. This game was important because of the gender mixing, and some of the players reported to Bill they played because they secretly liked certain members of the opposite sex.

Cliques

In activities in the classroom both during class time and the morning snack break, the children were also more gender segregated in second and third grade compared to first grade. However, it was only in Class B that there was both gender and status segregation with cliques that were clearly noticeable. In this class there was a small group of three girls who were looked up to by several of the other girls. This group often decided on activities during snack and outside play and would pass notes and get together to talk at every opportunity during class.

One day when Bill visited the class in third grade, the children had class pictures they had just received and were asking one another to sign their pictures on a blank page in a folder in which their picture was affixed. Bill noticed that all of the girls with the exception of Elisa were very concerned that they got the three leaders of the clique (Sonia, Federica, and Stella) to sign their names in their folders. Two of the boys asked Bill to sign his name and he did so, and after that almost all of the other children asked. However, Sonia instead of asking Bill herself sent Flora over to ask Bill to sign her folder rather than to bring it herself. Clearly, these girls relished their roles as leaders and liked to control others.

There was also a group of four boys in Class B who were quite exclusive in their interactions. Two of these boys, Alessandro and Leonardo, had been close friends since preschool (they did not attend the preschool we studied). At the start of third grade two new boys, Arturo and Claudio, joined Class B from another school. Bill was somewhat surprised to see that these boys had teamed up with the original two to form a solid clique, especially since Alessandro and Leonardo had been so resistant to the friendship attempts of Renato and Federico (the other two boys in the class) in first grade. These four were now always together during outside play where they frequently enjoyed disrupting the play of girls when not involved in their own soccer games. In class they often were talking and acting up. The teacher, Letizia, confided to Bill that the first two were hard enough, but now the four of them were a handful for her. Although the other three classes showed a pattern of general gender segregation and some close same-gender friendships, there were no sustained cliques as in Class B.

Best Friends

For the eight children we had interviewed from their time in preschool, there were few reported changes in their naming of best friends in second and third grade. They generally named same-gender friends in their class along with other same-gender friendships in other classes that they had first formed in preschool. The main exception to this pattern were Elisa and Renato in Class B who still reported some opposite-gender friends in and outside their class.

Group Identity

As noted previously, Bill was not able to visit the school for the children's fourth-grade year, but he did exchange letters with the kids. Nonetheless, while visiting the school for 6 weeks in 2001 when the children were in fifth grade, he was surprised by the overall blending of the four groups in activities outside their classrooms. The children were very relaxed with each other, often played across classes, and mixed together across the four groups at lunch and even during break time. All of a sudden it was as if they were no longer Classes A, B, C, or D, but fifth graders. This shift was encouraged by mixing children from all the classes in separate English classes and computer labs. However, the change mainly seemed to be the result of the children's recognition that they were now the oldest kids in the school. The younger children looked up to them, and the teachers gave them more responsibilities. The teachers had also prepared them for their last year at the school in numerous discussions, field trips, and other activities.

Some of these activities and events were directly related to the children's coming transition to middle school, which we will discuss in the next chapter. Others were more reflective than prospective as the children were reminded in certain tasks and discussions how much they had changed and matured in their 5 years at the school. Bill contributed to this feeling somewhat, as he now too was seen as a fifth grader and one of the oldest kids. During his fifth-year visit he brought a new digital camera to photograph the children in groups. Bill soon discovered that a couple of the children could operate the camera better than he could, so therefore he let them take the pictures and included himself within the various groups.

Later at an assembly for all the fifth graders, Bill used a school monitor and his computer to play some videotapes he had taken primarily during the first and second years at the school. The children were very happy to see themselves as first and second graders. Bill then displayed the new digital pictures by using a slide show graphics program on his computer. As he clicked through the pictures he passed through all the recent ones and then quite by accident started to display the pictures he had taken in second grade. The children laughed loudly when they saw the first picture of Carlotta. Bill asked if he should stop, and the children and teachers all yelled, "No!" So Bill continued and the children laughed loudly and shouted out at each picture noting how much they had changed in appearance since second grade. They especially enjoyed teasing the teachers when their pictures of 3 years ago were displayed even though the change in appearance was much less for the teachers. In this activity the children were getting a flashback to a time when they saw each other as young kids compared to the present when they were beginning to see each other as young women and men about to go on to a new phase in their lives.

Cross-Gender Relations

The mixing across classes in fifth grade was also accompanied by more interest in cross-gender relations. Both boys and girls talked about liking members of the opposite sex and having girlfriends and boyfriends, and Bill noticed that several of the kids had names of boyfriends and girlfriends in their notebooks. In Class C Bill noticed that Luciano had drawn a heart and printed the name, Stella, a girl in Class B inside. Bill was a bit surprised at this because Stella was in class B and Luciano would have little time to interact with her (pairs of classes, A with B and C with D, were more likely to carry out joint projects and be in English classes and computer and science labs together). Bill asked Luciano if he liked Stella. Luciano said he did, but he was not sure if Stella liked him. He said he saw her at lunch everyday and often on the playground and sometimes talked with her. Bill managed to sit next to Stella in Class B later, but saw no references to Luciano in her notebook. He felt that his involvement in Luciano's crush should stop there and did not directly question Stella.

Later during his time with the fifth graders, Bill joined a group of girls from all four classes on the outside playground. They were playing a game in which one girl would chant a phrase like, "Stella loves Luciano, is it true or not?" and "Elisa is through with Armando, true or false?" There was a lot of laughing in the group as they would yell out true or false, sometimes all agreeing and sometimes not. When there was disagreement, the girls debated evidence for their position (for example, "Elisa said it's true" or "Luciano sat next to Stella at lunch"). Bill observed for some time to see if the girls would react to his presence, and they just looked at him and smiled. Once when all the girls confirmed that a designated couple liked each other,

Bill asked if it was really true. The girls said it was true, but one girl, Irene, laughed and said, "It will not last."

This game, which Bill also observed on other days, never involved boys. If a boy passed by and commented on one of the proposals as being true or not, the girls quickly shooed him away. Also the girls being discussed were usually not present; on occasions when they were, they would often deny the relationship. Their denials, however, often involved smiling and laughter, as if they did not mind the attention. In a few instances a girl agreed she liked a certain boy, then added "*Ma allora!*" ("But so what!").

The children's behavior in these games as well as their secret crushes demonstrate that they are looking at cross-gender relationships in a new way. The findings are similar to those of Adler and Adler (1998), who studied preadolescents in the United States. Also the girls' games are very similar to findings by Evaldsson (1993), who studied Swedish elementary school children. Evaldsson found that children explored cross-gender relationships while playing jump rope in a game called Cradle of Love. By discussing who may like whom in these sorts of games, the pretend and real frames of the play are blurred, allowing the children to pursue real interests in the opposite sex, but in the safety of game or play.

INTERVIEWS WITH CHILDREN, PARENTS, AND TEACHERS

Our observations of changes in the nature of the school and peer culture (including children's friendships) over the course of the elementary school years were reinforced in interviews that we conducted with the elementary school teachers and a group of eight children and their parents. After the children completed first grade, we interviewed children, parents, and teachers three times, toward the end of the school year during second, third, and fifth grade. These interview data supplemented the observational data we discussed above and enabled us to trace the nature of the children's membership in the school and peer cultures, and also to analyze the different points of view shared by children and adults.

Children's Points of View

The interviews with the children focused on two areas: (1) their participation in and evaluation of classroom and educational activities and their relationships with their teachers; (2) their participation in peer culture related to their peer activities and friendships.

We first consider their perceptions related to their educational experiences. At the end of second grade, the eight children we interviewed said that they were happy with the school and that they liked most of the subjects. They did complain that a few subjects were difficult or boring (two children mentioned math, and one geography). They also reported some other things they did not like about school: They wanted to have more field trips, and they noted that being together with, and having to play with, children who were not close friends was sometimes unpleasant. The children did not think that they had too much homework, and they only seldom asked for their parents' help. Finally, as is often the case, the children also did not like to talk with their parents about what happened in school.

One year later, at the end of third grade, the answers to these questions were very similar: The children mainly liked school, and their preferences of subjects ranged from Italian to math, from gymnastics to music or history, while there were only a few responses about not liking math as much as other subjects. When we asked them to anticipate how Grades 4 and 5 would be, we collected some very interesting answers. The children did not express their fears about the possible difficulties that they might encounter, but instead they had developed a conception that expressed a parallel between their lives and the increasing demands of the school. One child, Elisa, stated that "everybody tells me that fifth grade is very difficult, but in my opinion it will be a normal class, we will be older, we will have more knowledge, and therefore we will all cope with it." Stefania referred to a sort of "theory" that she had developed during the first 3 years of elementary school, which went like this: "First grade is difficult because you have to learn everything, second grade is easy, third grade is a bit difficult, fourth grade will be easy, and fifth grade will be difficult because you have to pass an exam." However, she then concluded that the only thing one had to do was study and be well prepared.

These answers became more interesting and detailed in the interviews we collected at the end of fifth grade, when the children were nearing the transition to middle school. At the time of the interviews the children had already completed a visit to the middle school and had hosted a visit from the preschoolers who would be coming to first grade and be with their teachers in the coming year. All the interviewed children agreed that they liked elementary school for several reasons that are well synthesized in Elisa's answer: "I like elementary school for three reasons: because I made new friends, because I learned many new things, and because I got to know adults who will be for me a model when I will grow up." This reference to the relationship with adults as a main element of elementary school is quite surprising for a child and is also seldom mentioned in the literature. It may be related to the particular feature in Italian schools of keeping teachers and children together first throughout preschool and then in elementary school. In this way children get to know their teachers very well and form close relationships.

One question of the interview was centered about which year of elementary school they liked most. We had previously asked the same question of all the children who were currently attending fifth grade; we distributed a paper and asked them to write in an anonymous way which year they liked most and which one they liked least, and to give reasons for these choices. In total, 76 children answered. More than half of these children said that fifth grade was the year they preferred, and their reasons varied from the fact that they learned many interesting things to the recognition that they had reached a certain degree of maturity and were now entering adolescence. Many children also mentioned that, after 5 years spent together, they had become friends with everyone in their class. This observation fits with our earlier discussion and interpretation of our observations of the children in fifth grade. Only a few children liked second, third, or fourth grade most, while nearly 20 percent mentioned first grade as the best year, mainly because they met new friends and learned how to read and write.

Which year did the children like least? The more frequent answers were related to third and fourth grade. They did not like these two years because they felt that they were too difficult and they had too much homework. Only a few children mentioned fifth grade as the year they liked least, and the reason was mainly because it was too sad to say good-bye to friends who will not be in the same class in middle school.

When we asked the eight fifth-grade children we had been following since preschool to tell us which year they liked most, their answers were less homogeneous and varied a good deal. Between them, the children displayed positive opinions about all of the 5 years of elementary school. One girl chose first grade as the best because she met new classmates, new teachers, and it was an easy year. Another child preferred second grade because she had a math teacher that she really liked. A couple of children liked third grade because they had a lot of new things to learn—it was a difficult and challenging year. One boy was more favorable toward fourth grade because that was when boys and girls started playing together more often (we previously saw that this was an important factor in the peer culture). Finally, a few children said that fifth grade was the best year because they studied an interesting historical period (World War II) and also because they were happy about the way they were spending the last months together. Also in this interview near the end of fifth grade, the eight children especially reflected on their five years together and got a lot of attention from the teachers and younger children in the school. They dealt with some anxiety about the coming final exam, but also looked forward to several school and class parties, which would mark the end of their time at the elementary school in a joyous way.

Another question of the interviews at the end of fifth grade was centered on anticipation of middle school. We asked the children to tell us what they expected middle school would be like and if they were worried about the transition. Overall, the children said they were not worried about the coming transition and expressed a desire to meet new friends. They hoped that middle school would not be too difficult, that they would not have too much homework, and that the teachers would be nice. Stefania's answer was especially interesting because she remembered the hard time she had before and after the transition to elementary school (see Chapter 5). When we asked her to describe how she felt about the coming transition to middle school, she said, "I am very sad about it, because every time I finish one school and I face a transition, I feel very sick, and it is not easy for me." This answer shows how temporal dimensions are important for children, allowing them to anticipate future changes and prepare for these transitions in their lives.

As far as friendship and play were concerned in the last 3 years of elementary school, we asked the eight children we interviewed throughout the study to tell us who were their friends in school and to discuss their favorite activities. In the second and third grade most of the children named same-gender children as their friends; moreover, their friends came mostly from their own class, and were seldom the same friends they had in preschool. Even Elisa, who was very close with Michela in preschool, did not mention her as a friend in second grade. The class was the main reference point for friendship and play. Renato was an exception because, as we have discussed previously, he had trouble developing friendships with the other boys in his class, who had attended a different preschool together. In second grade, Renato mentioned as friends one boy and several girls, some of which were his classmates from preschool, while in third grade he explicitly stated that he did not like some of his classmates, especially Leonardo, who was always bullying him, and then he mentioned as friends two other boys of his class.

The answers to this question when the children were in fifth grade were much longer and more detailed. The children named more friends than they had in previous interviews. Sofia, for example, named all the children in her class as friends as well as several children from other classes. In fact, all the children named at least one child from another class and in most cases several. Also every child designated at least one child from preschool as a friend.

Another interesting pattern is that several children mentioned friends and then added which games they were playing together, and they also made reference to same- and opposite-gender friends. Consider, for example, the responses of Luciano and Elisa:

Luciano: I have some boyfriends, Giuseppe, Giovanni, Andrea, and Michele; then I have some girlfriends, Graziella, Alba, Caterina, and Susanna, well, we are all friends. With the girls, we mainly play some ball games, or *Strega Impalata* [a type of freeze tag involving a pretend witch] and we have a lot of fun.

Elisa: I like to play more with the girls than with the boys, it depends on the games we play; when we are with boys we like to play soccer.

These children's words are in line with the data we collected in the observations, since they show that after a long time spent together the peer culture was very well integrated, and the subgroups of boys and girls within the same class tended to fuse into one large group by fifth grade.

Parents' Points of View

Parents' evaluations of second grade were generally very positive. They all said they thought that their children were learning many things and that they liked the school and the teachers. They also reported that their children had few problem either with school requests or with friendship relations. Furthermore, they stated that their children were quite autonomous in doing their homework and that they talked a lot at home about what happened in school. These perceptions are very much in line with those of their children.

The parents' reports in third grade were quite different. In the Italian curriculum, third grade is considered to be a difficult year because the teachers start to teach history, geography, and science; thus the children have more to read at home and also have to learn how to report about these subjects when they are in school. At the end of third grade, when we asked parents if their children faced some difficulties in school, they mentioned a range of problems, including some learning difficulties; completing homework without help; experiencing some pressure and anxiety about school demands; and some problems in the relationship with the teachers. (For a discussion of the difficulties experienced by one child, Carlotta, see Corsaro, Molinari, & Rosier, 2002). Most parents reported changes that they noticed in their children during third grade, especially regarding the fact that they did not like talking about school and that they needed more help for doing their homework.

In fifth grade, parents' evaluations were mainly very positive. They described the physical changes their children were going through, and they were happy because children generally talked about what happened to them in school and with their friends. The long period of elementary school years together seems to be characterized, not only for children but also for parents, as having three distinct phases. First, they experience an easy period, lasting the first 2 years, when all members of the families are happy about school and do not complain about homework. Second, they have a more difficult time, which is clear at the end of third grade, depending both on the changing structure of school's curriculum and on the creation of subgroups within the peer culture. And finally, there is again a period of "inclusion," which reaches its height in the second half of fifth grade, when the children, very conscious of the fact that these will be the last months they spend together as a group, tend to re-create a mixed-gender peer culture (as in preschool) and to be very open to and participating in the school's culture.

What parents were more concerned about in fifth grade was the coming transition to middle school. This transition is relevant because of several changes both parents and children will have to cope with. First, the school's schedule will change: In middle school, children will come home at 1 P.M. (instead of 4:30 P.M.) and will not have lunch at school. As a result parents will have to prepare meals for their children and organize long afternoons when the children will be at home and most of the parents will be working. Second, homework will increase a lot, and will be related to many different subjects (children take 10 or 11 subjects in middle school), and this requires organization in autonomous reading and studying. Third, children will have new classmates (six out of the eight children we interviewed will go to the same school as the majority of their classmates, and for this reason they will be in a class where they will probably already know four or five children) and especially many new teachers. Middle school teachers teach one or two subjects, and therefore the children will have about eight teachers instead of two. Parents expressed their concerns about all of these issues. They hoped that their children would have an easy transition to middle school, as they mainly had from preschool to elementary school, but they expected it to be more difficult.

Teachers' Points of View

The data we collected in the interviews with the teachers at the end of second, third, and fifth grade were in line with how children and parents evaluated the cycle of elementary school. The teachers, in fact, stressed that second grade was a year when they deepened what they did in first grade, mainly working on reading and writing. Given the fact that the teachers stay with the same children for many years, they can take the opportunity to work hard one year, assuming that not all children will reach the objectives, and then work the following year mainly on improving and consolidating the children's skills and abilities.

All teachers described third grade as a very difficult year for the same reasons that children and parents pointed out, that is, they had to start teaching new subjects, and the children had to learn how to read and report on what they studied. One teacher, Arianna, stated, "Third grade is a particular class, it is a transition class, from first and second grade to fourth and fifth grade; we as teachers have the responsibility to establish the bases for learning methods of studying." All teachers said they were very tired at the end of third grade, and sometimes they felt exhausted and buried by responsibilities.

What teachers reported at the end of fifth grade was very different. They all seemed very touched about leaving the children they had been with for 5 years, and they also said that they believe it is very good to be with the same children for 5 years, which is somewhat contrary to what they told us at the end of first grade (see Chapter 8). Consider what one teacher, Renata, said:

> At the end of 5 years with the children I am always somehow touched; I don't like the idea of leaving them; in fact I always make jokes. I say: "Now that you are really good I will not be your teacher anymore." But it's true, when you finally reach the time that you can really work well with them, it's time for them to move to a new school.

Another teacher, Giusi, discussed how she conceptualized the whole cycle of elementary school:

> To be truthful, this is how I consider these 5 years. First grade has been a wonderful year, we were working very well together; second grade was a quiet year; but third grade was really hard, for me and for the children, we were all very tired at the end of the year. Then in fourth grade we all recovered, and now in fifth grade I feel we are closing just as we began, in a wonderful way.

Successes and challenges for teachers in the different grades related to two different aspects: On one side, teachers worked hard from the beginning to help children to form friendships and to establish good relationships with the teachers; and on the other side, their aims were to make children interested in learning, and to stimulate their curiosity toward knowledge. At the end of fifth grade they all seemed satisfied with both these challenges, and they expressed their confidence that the children were well prepared for middle school, especially because they like what they do in school. This is what Arianna said in the interview:

> I think they [the children] are ready for middle school, because they are curious, they have enthusiasm, they want to learn new things, to understand what is taught to them, they are motivated and stimulated in school.

Overall, the teachers agreed about the importance of priming events for the transition to middle school. They especially considered the visit to middle school as important, as well as other events that helped the children to anticipate future changes, like some discussions they had about sexuality and changes in feelings and emotions.

What teachers were disappointed with, especially as a final evaluation at the end of fifth grade but also in the previous interviews, was the relationship with the parents. This is somehow discrepant with what the parents told us in the interviews, where they mainly expressed positive judgments about the teachers. The main problem in the relationship between parents and teachers was attributed by the teachers to the fact that parents were very interested and participated in all meetings when they were called upon to discuss their own child face-to-face, but they were not very much involved at a more collective level, when school or class projects were to be carried on. In this respect, their words reflect a general idea about the changes in societies, from a collectivistic orientation to a more individualistic one. When the teachers stay with the same children for 5 years and then start with a new group, they can easily note the sharp differences that have occurred in those 5 years, and their expectations about families can be somewhat disappointing.

Chapter 10

Priming Events for the Transition to Middle School

After 5 years in elementary school, the children would be moving on to middle school for 3 years. This move involves a major transition in the children's lives because middle school in Italy is very different from elementary school. Children take 10 or 11 subjects and usually have about eight teachers, each of whom teaches one or two subjects. Middle schools are normally larger than elementary schools and are operated on half-day morning schedules 6 days a week. Therefore, children would experience a number of changes in the transition from elementary to middle school.

As was the case in the transition from preschool to elementary school, the children participated in several formal priming activities and events as well as many informal ones in preparation for the transition. Basic elements in the school structure, educational curriculum, and relationship between teachers, students, and parents that existed at the end of preschool were also present in the final months of elementary school. These elements were key to the children's collective participation in priming events.

In this chapter we first examine a number of activities and events, which took place when the children were in fifth grade, that were central in their preparation for the transition to middle school. These events ranged from formal visits to the middle school to the reception for preschoolers visiting the elementary school, to preparing for and taking a final exam, to special parties arranged by parents and teachers, to a citywide activity for all fifth graders noting their special status and coming transition, to informal traditions in the elementary school that were more under the control of the children themselves.

After examining these priming events and comparing them to similar events that took place in the last year of preschool, we go on to examine interview data of the same eight children and their parents at the end of the children's second year of middle school. In the interviews the children and parents reflect on the children's transitions and their adaptation to middle school and compare them to earlier educational experiences. Finally, the interviews provide a brief glimpse into the children's and their parent's anticipation of the future transition to high school, which involves a major decision regarding the children's educational trajectories and eventual places in the adult world.

PRIMING EVENTS

In the last chapter we noted that the children were both excited and relaxed during Bill's visit to the elementary school in the last weeks of fifth grade. During these last weeks the children participated in a number of activities that marked the ending of their time in elementary school and prepared them for transition to middle school. Thus we see these activities as priming events. The children looked forward to most of these activities with great anticipation. However, a few of the activities were somewhat threatening to the children and provoked mild anxiety.

Visits to the Middle School

The middle school that most of the children graduating from Giacomo Puccini elementary school would attend was just a short walk away from their school. Bill accompanied Classes A and D on their separate visits to the middle school in late May 2001. As Class A approached the school, we could see obvious differences between the middle and elementary schools. The school was a somewhat larger building than the elementary school and had a large parking area for the teachers' cars in front of the building. The school was surrounded by grass with a concrete walkway between the two main buildings making up the school. Unlike the elementary school, the middle school had no fenced-in outside play area or playground equipment.

After we entered the school, we were greeted and escorted to a large meeting room where we were met by the school principal who welcomed the children with a short speech. Then two teachers and several middle school children served as guides to show us around the school. When we first entered, things were very quiet as classes were in session, but as we left the meeting room, the tranquil atmosphere had changed dramatically. There was now a break between classes, and children filled the hallways, talking loudly, laughing, and playfully pushing and shoving. The noise level was much higher than during break time in elementary school. Also the middle school children seemed so much bigger and older. It was a bit intimidating for the elementary school kids, but they stuck with their guides and moved into a music room.

Once in the large music room the outside noise was blocked out, and we could see that many of the middle school children in the class had already taken their seats and were unpacking their instruments. Bill and the elementary school children and their teacher sat with their guides on some steps along the far side of the room. Soon the class began. The music teacher welcomed the visitors and said the class would play some pieces they had been working on. The children all played similar instruments (flutes and recorders) and the two songs were well done and the elementary school children applauded in appreciation. There were no formal music classes that involved playing instruments in elementary school, so the children got some insight into a new activity and type of training they would encounter in middle school.

After the music room the group visited a woodshop, electronics lab, and a chemistry lab. Again these were all new experiences for the children as no such labs existed in the elementary school. The middle school teacher explained what went on in these labs as there were no classes present during the visit. The student guides also described some projects they did in the labs and pointed to some work they completed in the woodshop. The middle school children joked around a bit and were corrected by the teacher, who told one of the boys to return to class. The elementary school children were impressed by the labs and seemed a bit anxious about the disciplining of the middle school students by the teacher.

After leaving the labs there was another break in classes, and the group stopped in the hallway. The middle school teacher allowed the older students to take some of the visiting children around to look at various parts of the open areas in the school. Unlike the elementary school, the middle school had some vending machines for students, and the middle school students had more freedom to talk, joke, and engage in physical play in the hallways compared to elementary school.

When classes resumed, we briefly visited another music room and then returned to the meeting room where the tour began. The guide asked the elementary school children if they had any questions, and several children spoke up. Paola asked about school rules and if the teachers often had to discipline the children. This question seemed related to the earlier incident when one of the student guides was disciplined. Carla asked if there were many exams and if they were hard or easy. The middle school teacher said that there were more exams than in elementary school, but students did well if they studied and prepared. Viviana asked about the composition of groups in the classes. She seemed concerned about whether she would be able to keep some of her friends from elementary school with her in the same classes. The middle school teacher seemed prepared for this question and said there would be three groups of children who took all classes together for all 3 years of middle school. He noted that the actual composition of the groups was not decided until shortly before school started.

After this meeting the group was joined by one of the language teachers, who spoke to Bill in English and took the group to the language classrooms. English and French were taught in this middle school, and each student's desk in this modern classroom was equipped with a tape deck and microphone for practicing speaking and comprehension. The children and Bill were very impressed with this room. A number of the elementary school children conversed in English with the teacher and said how much they liked learning a new language.

Finally, the English teacher took the group to the gym, which was connected to the main building by a second floor walkway or bridge. The gym was much bigger than the small one in Giacomo Puccini. We arrived at a sort of balcony and looked down at two full basketball courts, one of which was set up for volleyball and some students were in the midst of a game. The elementary school children were quite excited and called down to those playing below who looked up and waved. Next we went into a room on the second level which contained a climbing wall. Several middle school students were using ropes to climb the wall. They offered to help the elementary school children climb, and several took up the offer; all were very impressed with this facility. Soon after visiting the gym, the group returned to elementary school. The children talked to each other very excitedly on the way back. They had anticipated seeing all the older children, but were surprised by all the different labs, the music and language classrooms, and especially the gym.

In the days following the class visits the children talked with their teachers about what they saw and what they thought it would be like in middle school. Most of the children were confident that they were ready to attend middle school and noted they felt older and more mature just by making the visit. A few children expressed worries about finding the right classroom and having so many different teachers. The elementary school teachers reassured them they would soon find their way around and pointed to the fact that they had done very well going to their own English classes and using the computer lab. Several children noted they might not get to see some of their best friends very often and said they would miss their teachers who had become very important in their lives in the last 5 years. This anticipated separation from peers and especially from the elementary school teachers was a central element of many of the other priming events which occurred in the last weeks of elementary school.

Visit of the Preschoolers

On the day of the visit of the preschoolers to the elementary school, Bill could not believe that 5 years had passed so quickly. Now as he saw preschool teachers arrive with a new group of 5-year-olds, he found himself on the receiving and nourishing end of this ritual and important priming event. The nature of the visit had changed little over the 5-year period. A central element was the leadership role of the fifth graders who relished the opportunity to talk with and reassure the young preschoolers about coming to first grade. They took them all around their classrooms and into many other areas of the school. Again there was a party outside where the fifth graders served food and they and their teachers sang songs with the visiting preschoolers. Looking in the faces of the fifth graders, Bill could feel their memories of when they had first come to the elementary school, which was now so familiar and like home to them. In this ritual, like all rites of passage, there are both retrospective and prospective elements. The fifth graders in talking with and entertaining the preschoolers thought back on their 5 years in the school and literally relived some elements as they pointed to an artistic display, worked with the young preschoolers in the computer lab, and talked about field trips and other school projects. At the same time, such retrospection so soon after their own visit to the middle school reminded the fifth graders that their time in the elementary school was coming to an end. It was a happy and somewhat sad recognition as the fifth grade had been a year when they felt special. Now it was time to move on to new challenges, new peers, and a new chapter in their lives.

Final Exam

In Italy there is a system of statewide final exams at the end of elementary school, middle school, and high school that must be passed before a student can move on to the next level. Anxiety about these exams, most especially the one at the end of high school that provides the possibility of starting university is very much a part of the public educational culture in Italy. Still, Bill was surprised at how anxious even some of the very best elementary school children were about the exam they would take over a few days after the end of the school year.

The teachers assured the children and their parents that students were well prepared for the exam. It was also a well-known fact among the parents that, except in very exceptional cases, all elementary school students pass the exam. Nonetheless, many of the children constantly questioned the teachers about the exam and expressed worries that they would forget what they had learned when it came time to take the exam.

The exam normally occurs over several days and has an oral part on one morning and written parts for Italian, math, and English on three mornings. On the day of the oral part of the exam Bill did not enter the classrooms as not to disturb the process in any way. Instead he waited outside the school until the exam was over because it lasted only for the morning session. While Bill waited a number of the parents of the fifth-grade children arrived and were also waiting for their children to finish. The first child to come out of the school after finishing the exam was Marina, from Class A, whom Bill had known since preschool. She saw Bill and ran up to him and said, "*Bill, era molto facile!*" ("Bill, it was very easy!"). She then ran off to give her mother a hug and asked if she could wait to talk with other children when they finished.

Soon many other children came out and also reported that this first oral part of the exam was easier than they had expected. Soon the outside yard was filled with fifth graders who laughed, talked, and played. They were all very relieved at having finished part of the exam and now began to see themselves as ready for middle school. The experience of taking the first in a series of such exams is a priming event not only for the transition to middle school but also for the exam system itself, which is so important in both the peer and adult culture.

End-of-the-Year Parties and Sports Day

As was the case in the preschool, there were end-of-the-year parties for the whole school and individual classes in elementary school. These parties took on special significance for the fifth graders and their families. With the transition to middle school many friendships among the children, among the children and parents, and among parents would be altered and curtailed. Thus the fifth-grade children and their parents played a major role in the planning and conducting of the general end-of-the-year party in their final year at the school in June 2001. The party had many entertaining activities for the children, but the one we remember the most was what we call the "surprise box" sale. When Bill arrived early the night of the big party, which was held in the outside yard of the school, one of the parents quickly grabbed him by the arm and led him inside the school. "We need your help in getting all the boxes outside in the booth," said Silvia, the mother of a girl in Class A. She led Bill to a room in the school which was filled with boxes of all shapes and sizes that had been expertly wrapped in shiny paper.

The first thing Bill thought was some parents had already done a lot of work in getting all these boxes to the school, placing gifts inside, and wrapping all the boxes. Once in the room another parent filled Bill's open arms with several boxes. Bill carried them outside and handed them to yet other parents who were stacking the boxes in a booth where a sign noted that any child could buy a box for a nominal amount of money. The sign also indicated that every box contained a gift, and some contained special surprise gifts that were worth well more than the purchase price.

Bill marveled at this Italian version of a Wishing Well or Grab Bag booth he had seen at school fund-raisers and county fairs in the United States. However, he had little time to ask about it because he was pulled away to bring out more boxes. Once the party started, Bill bought a box for his daughter, which contained a small trinket. He also hung around the booth and watched his fellow fifth graders make purchases and rejoiced with a few who won special gifts as well as those who were happy with their less costly surprises.

There was also lots of food and drink at the party and several different kinds of games. Many of the parents talked to Bill and said their children would miss him. In this way he shared in their community of friendships with each other and with their children. The kids were having too good a time to be as reflective as Bill, the parents, or the teachers. However, a few came to join Bill alone or with their parents to talk and share memories.

In addition to the final school party, the fifth-grade classes also had their own parties. Classes A, B, and C had parties at the school where parents brought food and drink. After the dinner, the parents mingled and talked while the children ran and played in the play yard together for a last time. Class D arranged a more formal dinner for which they rented a restaurant slightly out of town in the countryside. Bill was invited and sat with a group of fathers at a large table and enjoyed the wonderful multicourse meal served family style. The fathers had many questions for Bill about his time in the school, his research, his family, and the United States. It was a bit overwhelming even if Bill's Italian had been fluent, but he did the best he could and enjoyed all the attention. He had more fun after dessert, however, running around and playing games with the kids in an open area outside the restaurant. At the end of the evening there were many toasts and a special gift for Giusi, the teacher in Class D for the children's 5 years. The present was a beautiful blouse and Giusi was very touched and was crying a little as she expressed her gratitude to the parents for their thoughtfulness.

Both the general end-of-the-year party for the school and the separate parties for the fifth-grade classes capture the high value placed on social interaction, community, and civil society that is so evident in Modena and more generally in Italy. The other event that captured this civil society was the special *Scuola Sport* (Sports School) that was held in a large park for all fifth graders in Modena. Bill attended the event on a beautiful Saturday in late May a few weeks before the end of the school year.

The Sports School activity was organized by groups of volunteers who ranged in age from high school students to retired senior citizens. The event began as all the fifth graders gathered with their fellow students from each of the elementary schools in the city in front of a small stage that was covered with colorful balloons.

Once the children were all grouped together they were led in a group song with coordinated movements. Then the children were told they could go to join one of over 20 different areas. In each area a different sport was presented and described by volunteers, and children could then join in and participate in the particular sport. Sports that were represented were wind surfing, field hockey, fishing, baseball, judo, boxing, canoeing, and many others.

The fifth graders had a great time moving from area to area and receiving instructions and trying out the different sports. Bill walked around with a group of parents from Giacomo Puccini to watch and cheer on the children. Near the end of the event three men parachuted into the park and landed successfully in an area near the center of the activities. Like the event itself, this demonstration was impressive and a lot of fun.

The *Scuola Sport*, like the special concert performed by these same children when they were five-year-olds and finishing preschool, was a citywide activity that celebrated the children's lives at an important rite of passage, in this case, the completion of elementary school. It was an activity the children looked forward to and very much enjoyed. It was also a priming event in that it again impelled the children to look forward to their coming transition to a new stage in their lives and their participation in the Modena community.

Chaos in the Lunchroom

On what was to Bill's mind the last full day of school before the final exam, Fabrizio, from Class D told him, "Bill, be sure to come to lunch with us on Monday!" Bill was confused by Fabrizio's invitation because he thought on the day in question there would be no lunch as the students would only be in school a half day to take their final exam. But Fabrizio assured Bill that there was one more full day of school. He also seemed very excited that Bill be there for lunch. Bill had already been surprised with the birthday party in his honor, so he figured that perhaps something special was to happen on the last day of lunch.

As it turned out, something special did happen, and Bill was glad that Fabrizio invited him. Things started out in the regular way as Bill made his way to the lunchroom with Class D, joining Fabrizio and other kids at one of the fifth-grade tables. The children seemed very keyed up, but Bill thought it was just the excitement of the last day of school.

During lunch there was a lot of visiting by different children from all four fifth-grade classes from table to table. The children were laughing and joking, and the women who served the lunch also seemed to be in a good mood. Bill sensed something was up when he heard some shouting. Luciano, a boy from Class C, had sneaked up behind Elisa from Class B and poured a glass of water down her back.

Then the chaos began as all the children began filling their glasses with water and throwing it at their neighbors. Bill looked to the teachers who had backed out into the hallway with smiles on their face. About that time Sandra, who had loved to tease Bill ever since preschool, came up and said, "Just for you, Bill, a glass of water," and flung the water in Bill's face and all over his shirt. Bill then went to get some water to retaliate, but found the plastic pitcher empty. But then he saw the women who served food bringing in more full pitchers of water and setting them on the table and laughing.

The water fight was now in full force, and Bill was surprised when the women who worked in the lunch room were also involved. They chased down several of the children pouring water down their back, and one of the women even threw water at Bill. There was shouting, screaming, and laughter, and everyone was all wet. Then someone announced, "Uh-oh, it's the director!" And there stood the school director in his immaculate suit and tie surveying the scene with a stern look on his face. Everyone stopped throwing water, and the room grew silent. Then to Bill's surprise the director smiled and then turned and left the lunchroom without a word.

After the director left, the teachers returned and the water throwing ended. The children gathered around the women who had served them lunch for 5 years and gave them good-bye hugs. Each of the women also gave Bill a hug good-bye, and again Bill felt like one of the fifth graders.

On the way out Fabrizio said, "That was a lot of fun, wasn't it, Bill?" Bill agreed and thought to himself that this "chaos in the lunchroom" was probably a yearly event for the fifth graders that was very well orchestrated by the teachers, lunchroom staff, and the director. He also thought that the creation and acceptance of disorder was a very interesting way to mark the end of one's participation in the social order of an organization. It also clearly broke down the mounting tension about the final exam.

CHILDREN'S AND PARENTS' PERCEPTION OF TRANSITION AND ADAPTATION TO MIDDLE SCHOOL

At the end of the second year of middle school, we interviewed all eight children we had been following since preschool, and seven parents. The interviews were again carried out in their homes, and all the children and families were happy to participate once again. The interviews were much shorter than those collected during preschool or elementary school, and were aimed at understanding how the children and their parents described middle school as well as the nature of the transition and adaptation to the new level of schooling.

Although most of the children had made a relatively smooth transition from preschool to elementary school, almost all the children and their parents described the transition to middle school as characterized by difficulties of various types. Consider, for example, what children answered to the question related to which year (first or second) of middle school they preferred. Seven out of eight children said they preferred the second year, because in the first one "you are the youngest in the school, and everybody is teasing you," or because "during the second year we are all friends in my class," or because "the first year has been difficult, we had to learn how it worked, now it is much easier."

The children did not complain about homework or the school's organization (going to school on Saturdays, having to study many subjects every day). However, they were not enthusiastic about school, especially in reference to some teachers who did not seem interested in developing relationships with students.

When asked about subjects they preferred, most of the children (six of the eight) mentioned English and other foreign languages. This finding is interesting in that the study of English is now seen as very important in Italian education. Also these children were first introduced to English in preschool, and they all very much liked their English teachers during the last 3 years of elementary school. Here we see important continuity regarding language training and the importance of early introduction to English in preschool. The finding suggests that it would be useful to have English instruction from the start of elementary school.

When asked about whether they made field trips in middle school, all the children named a few and said they were enjoyable. However, they also said that there were many fewer field trips than in elementary school. All of the children noted that this was related to an overall pattern of more work and fewer entertaining, playful activities than in elementary school and preschool. In fact, Luciano said he did not like middle school because it was too much work and that his favorite subject was gym (or physical education) because in this class there was at least some time for fun. On the other hand, Luciano and his mother noted the importance of study and work in middle school and said that he was adapting well.

Finally, the children's responses to their friendship relations in middle school were interesting. All eight children reported as good friends children they had first met in both preschool and elementary school. The fact that friendships first established in preschool were still important in the children's lives is a sign of the continuity of peer relations and culture fostered by the preschool system in Modena. It is also reinforced by keeping children together over several years in the same groups of peers for both preschool and elementary school. Thus, when they reach middle school, the demands of more intense study, many new teachers, and new peers is tempered by the continuation of close friendships made at a very young age. In fact, for one boy, Renato, the renewal of a friendship with Lorenzo, a boy he first met in preschool who did not attend his elementary school, was important in his adjustment to middle school.

Like their children, the parents also found the transition to middle school was more demanding than the transition from preschool to elementary school. They often referred to the fact that their son or daughter was in a difficult age period, preadolescence, and that this was one of the things that made middle school difficult. As for the transition, one mother stated that it was very hard because "at the end of elementary school they are still children, and after 3 months they are supposed to be much more mature, but they are not, and therefore they feel very strange and somehow lost." Almost all parents agreed that their children were very well prepared for this transition, except for the major difference in the type of relationship between teachers and children. In elementary school teachers and children were very close, but in middle school the time for human relations was more limited. Therefore, from the parents' perspective the teachers seemed colder and more distant from the students compared to elementary school and especially preschool.

Parents were also conscious about the fact that there was less continuity between elementary and middle school than between preschool and elementary school. The gap between the two schools, in terms of learning requirements, organization, and relationships with teachers and between classmates, was very large. As a result the children took several months to understand how to deal with these differences. The parents also expressed some regret that they could not participate in the life of the school in the ways they did in elementary school and especially in preschool. Finally, the parents were all a bit nervous about the fact that in one year's time their children would have to decide on the type of high school (in terms of area of concentration of study) they would attend. Sonia's mother, in particular, felt that this decision was made difficult by the short period of only 3 years of middle school. She felt more time was needed to make such an important decision.

Overall, as we have tracked a group of Italian children through two important transitions (preschool to elementary school and elementary to middle school), we have found a great deal of continuity and satisfaction on the part of both children and parents. However, it is clear that both the parents and children were less relaxed about the next transition to high school, which was made more complex and challenging due to the need in Italy of choosing a particular area of concentration of studies.

PART IV

Applying Key Findings to Early Education Policy and Practice

CHAPTER 11

Summing Up and Looking Ahead in Italian Early Education

In this book we investigated the early life transitions of Italian children through a 7-year longitudinal ethnography. The study began with Bill's entry into the school and peer cultures of a group of children in their third year in a *scuola dell'infanzia* in Modena, Italy. We noted the many positive features of the Modena preschool system and its favorable comparison to that of the city of Reggio Emilia which has been documented as having one of the best and progressive preschool programs in the world (Cadwell, 1997, 2003; Edwards, Gandini, & Forman, 1998). Bill's observations and participation in the school and peer cultures of a group of 5–6-year-olds during their final 6 months in a Modena preschool we call Giuseppe Verdi reveal many of the positive aspects—long-term projects, children's artwork and use of graphic language, the engagement of children's ideas and opinions, documentation of collective practices and projects, high family involvement—that have been praised by American early education scholars in regard to Reggio Emilia schools (see Katz, 1998). What we added to this earlier work is a more intensive focus on the children's peer relations and their incorporation of the life and quality of the school into their own peer culture over their 3 years together in the school.

After becoming part of this group of 21 children, Bill then documented formal and informal priming events—like visits to the elementary school and literacy projects that instilled an interest in and orientation to reading and writing—that helped pave the way for their transition to elementary school. Also through observations in the peer culture and interviews with children and their parents, we captured the children's thoughts, representations, and emotions regarding the coming transition during the summer months after they completed preschool.

An especially unique aspect of our study is that we then made the actual transition with the children to Giacomo Puccini the elementary school that 17 of the 21 children attended. Bill observed in the four first-grade classes on a regular basis from the start of school in early September to mid-December 1996. In elementary school the group he observed increased to 80 children. Again we documented the school and peer culture in each class and charted what was generally a smooth transition to elementary school. We identified similar features in the structure and curriculum of the preschool and elementary school—especially the practice of keeping children together in the same group with the same teachers, the reliance on long-term projects, daily engaged discussions with the children, and the use of artwork or graphic language to supplement and help develop reading and writing skills. We also documented peer relations in the first grade as the children went about keeping old friends and making new ones. We continued to carry out interviews with a sample of 8 children and their parents from the preschool throughout elementary school and even into middle school.

After becoming part of the first-grade classes, Bill kept in touch with the children, when he was not in Modena, through cards, letters, and e-mails and also returned in spring of 4 years of elementary school for 6-week periods of participant observation. In this way Bill shared in the children's collective involvement in the school and peer culture over all 5 years of elementary school. Thus we were able to document not only the children's transition to but also their participation and progress in elementary school.

Finally, through participation in priming events—like visits to the middle school, end-of-the-year parties, and community-wide activities designed especially for fifth graders—as well as through interviews with teachers and some parents and children, we were able to document and gain a sense of the children's transition and adaptation to middle school.

KEY FACTORS IN TRANSITIONS

This intensive longitudinal study captured the nature and quality of life of this group of children during these important educational transitions. We not only documented the nature of educational processes and children's learning, but also the children's evolving membership in a changing peer culture, their lives as students, and the role of their families in these early educational institutions. Overall, we found that the children's experiences were highly positive and that their educational achievement and social development showed continuity and marked progress and maturity in their relations with peers, parents, teachers, and other adults in their community.

Features of Positive Transitions

There were a number of key features that supported smooth and positive transitions to and success in elementary school. Several of these are related to educational structure, policy, and practice in Modena. First, all children making the transition had experienced high-quality preschool education which promoted the positive development of cognitive, social, and literacy skills. Although the children varied somewhat in their strengths and weaknesses in these skills, they all began first grade with a strong foundation for learning and progressing to new levels of knowledge and skills.

Second, the continuity of a structure of keeping children together in the same group with the same teachers for the whole period of education contributed positively to a smooth transition to and progress in elementary school. The children identified and bonded with their new teachers and classmates early on, knowing that they would be together throughout elementary school. The teachers knew and took advantage of the fact that they had ample time to work with children who had different needs both academically and socially. This structure of keeping children together also contributed to each student's attachments to their group or class and over time to their particular grade (from first through fifth) as they progressed through elementary school.

Third, the close coordination and cooperation of preschool and elementary school teachers in our study contributed to positive transitions. The preschool teachers met several times with the elementary school teachers and discussed their classes and individual students. The preschool teachers shared dossiers of each child with the elementary school teachers. These dossiers marked the child's strengths and weaknesses at the time of transition.

Fourth, the strong parental involvement in the preschool years encouraged and prepared parents for supporting their children's transition to elementary school. It was clear from our interviews that parents were aware of their children's strengths and weaknesses because of their intricate knowledge of the preschool educational program. Many parents and children also turned to older siblings or older siblings of friends as models for the transition process. We also found that once the children were in first grade, the older children took an active role in break periods to check up on their siblings and friends to help ease the transition to the new level of education. It is clear that these actions were encouraged and supported by the elementary school teachers in the first months of the transition process.

Some Problematic Aspects of Transitions

As we discussed in Chapter 8, the teachers reported that some children had trouble with the transition to first grade. In two cases these problems involved children who had been very good students in preschool and, in fact, often took leadership roles in various school and peer activities. One problem these children faced in first grade was that they were not given as much attention as they had become accustomed to in preschool. In the case of one girl, Elisa, the problem was minor, and she quickly adapted to the new situation in the first months of elementary school. For Luciano, however, problems with behavior in class and academic performance persisted into the middle years of elementary school. Luciano often acted out in class and his teacher noted that he was a bit of a perfectionist and slow to finish his work. She worked with him and his mother, and there was a dramatic improvement in fourth and fifth grades; in fact, the teacher reported Luciano had become a model student.

These cases illustrate that the structure of children staying together for 3 years in preschool can build high expectations for some students when they move on to the bigger and more academically demanding elementary school. However, given the children's abilities, teacher involvement, and parent and teacher relations, the problems were not long lasting.

A second problematic aspect relates to social relations and the development of exclusive cliques in one of the classes in particular. Here the practice of keeping children together, especially during the 3 years of preschool, led to a solidification of certain cliques and some problems for those children who were excluded. One boy, Renato, who had strong friendship bonds with several children in preschool found it difficult to become friends with a group of boys in his class who had gone to a different preschool. Renato dealt with this problem by interacting with girls in his class and some former male friends from preschool in other classes. Eventually the problem dissipated, but Renato, his parents, and his teacher noted it was difficult for him and affected his school work to some degree in first and second grade.

Finally, there were other problems related to the practice of keeping children together. When strong class communities are formed over several years of teachers and students being together, even brief or minor changes can be disruptive. In the elementary school there was some disruption in two of the classes given the rather frequent change in math and special education teachers even though the Italian teacher remained the same throughout the 5 years. Also the Italian teacher in Class D had an extensive sick leave in the third year which several parents felt raised difficulties for their children (see Corsaro, Molinari, & Rosier, 2002).

Overall Evaluation of Transition and Generalizability

Despite some ups and downs and bumps in the road for a number of the children, in general we saw that these Italian children's experiences in elementary school were as rich and rewarding as those in preschool. It is not just that the children receive excellent preschool education, which is carried over to positive experiences and outcomes in elementary school. These experiences (along with the children's involvement in a rich civic society in Modena) enriched these children's childhoods and gave them a sense of participatory power and pride in their schools, their peer groups, their families, and their community.

Since this is a relatively small case study we cannot generalize the findings we detailed in the previous chapters to all of Italy or even the Emilia-Romagna region. However, we feel confident that that the preschool and elementary school we studied were representative of the overwhelming majority of schools in Modena. Also the events making up civic society involving children in Modena were impressively organized, traditional, and well attended. However, only further research in other Italian cities can help us estimate the overall quality of early education in the country and its contribution to the quality of young children's lives during these important early transitions.

CONTRIBUTIONS TO THEORY ON CHILDREN'S LIFE TRANSITIONS

In Chapter 2 we reviewed the various theoretical perspectives that guided our ethnographic study of these Italian children's transitions in the early education system. We stressed the importance of three interrelated theoretical approaches: interpretive reproduction, sociocultural theory, and life course theory. Here we briefly situate our findings in line with these theories and discuss how our research has benefited from and contributed to these theories.

Interpretive Reproduction

Interpretive reproduction stresses children's collective agency in their evolving membership in their culture while at the same time acknowledging that children are affected and constrained by features of the wider culture or society of which they are members (Corsaro, 1992, 2005). Central to interpretive reproduction is a focus on local peer cultures that children create and participate in as they make transitions to and participate in cultural institutions like families and schools. It was within peer cultures that the children collectively participated in priming events that prepared them for and supported them during the transitions from preschool to elementary school and from elementary school to middle school.

In some cases these priming events were formally designed by adults (teachers and parents) to signify that the children were completing one phase in the educational process and were about to begin another. Formal visits to the new schools in the spring of their final year first in preschool and then in elementary school are clear examples of such priming events. Although designed and controlled by teachers, children participated in these priming events as groups of peers with a long history (3 years in preschool and 5 years in elementary school). This shared peer culture was important to what they took from these priming events both in terms of their conceptualization of the coming transition and their later adaptation to and progress in the new institution. Other formal priming events designed by families (such as end-of-the-year parties) were also experienced with friends and peers with whom they shared enduring relationships and memories of past everyday routines and special activities and events. During these celebrations of transition or rites of passage, these past experiences provided a camaraderie that crystallized free-floating emotions and memories of what the children had shared and anticipations, fears, and expectations of what their lives would be like in a new educational institution.

The peer group was important in a variety of other, more informal priming events that were more under the control of the children themselves. In preschool, for example, with each other and with Bill, who had become an accepted member of the group, the children tried out and evaluated their developing literacy skills in peer play and in their printing and writing in Bill's notebook. Here the everyday play routines of peer culture were supplemented by activities that were forward looking and center around new skills that the children saw as central to their coming lives as elementary school students. At the end of elementary school, the children devised their own rite of passage in their collective taking over of the lunch room. Although this rite was no doubt influenced by their witnessing of a similar event by fifth graders the year before, it was still something that they could call their own, and it marked the coming to an end of their participation in the general order of the elementary school through the creation of disorder. It was a very special disorder because not only were the children clearly violating school etiquette and rules, but they did it with the implicit (teachers and director) and explicit (the lunchroom workers) support of school authorities. The event was not only a rite of passage but again one of priming because through the very nature of their participation the children not only reflected on and celebrated their group's time and experiences in the elementary school, but they were also forced to recognize that they must now move on to a new institution with a new set of rules and regulations. In the midst of their creation of disorder they look ahead to a new social order, which they must learn, adapt to, and quite possibly come to challenge.

Sociocultural Theory

Patterns in our findings regarding the children's transitions also can be interpreted in line with features of sociocultural theory as seen in Rogoff's work. Our focus in studying the transition process was on what Rogoff sees as sociocultural activities that are collectively produced rather than the experiences or changes in individuals (Rogoff, 1996, 2003). We observed children's sociocultural activities in the preschool, during the transition to elementary school, and in elementary school on what Rogoff calls "three planes of analysis" (individual, interpersonal, and community).

Although most of our observations focused on the interpersonal plane (collective activities in the school and peer cultures), we did at times shift the lens of the focus of the analysis to the individual and to the community. For example, in observations and in interviews with teachers and parents, we noted specific problems and also positive change and progress in individual children. As we discussed earlier, we found especially during the first-grade year that some children, such as Elisa and Luciano, who had very good experiences in preschool and who were seen as leaders by the first-grade teachers had adjustment problems in first grade.

Additionally in a set of observations and interviews we traced the progress and problems of one girl, Carlotta, during her transition to elementary school and during the elementary school years (also see Corsaro, Molinari, & Rosier, 2002). Overall, Carlotta's transition to and progress in elementary school went well, but she did have some ups and downs. Still, Carlotta was a very active member of her class throughout elementary school, as she had been in preschool, and we know from interviews that she made a smooth transition to middle school.

In these examples where the focus was on individual children in the changing nature of sociocultural activities in the transition process, we observed that it was not just the individual children who were changing and adjusting, but also the teachers and to some extent the children's peers. Despite some temporary problems the overall nature of the transition at the interpersonal level was positive over time. Because of the temporary discontinuity, these particular individual children stand out. Other children, however, who we expected might have transition problems because they were very quiet and somewhat less advanced academically in preschool, blossomed in elementary school where they did not hold back and look for other childen to model as they did in preschool. In a new group where these former leaders were not present, these children struck out on their own in actively participating in classroom activities and in establishing new friends in the peer culture.

We also, at times, focused on the community plane in our analysis of transition processes. Here events that on the surface look like celebrations of past accomplishments or rites of passage, such as the graduation party from preschool and end-of-the-year parties after fifth grade, take on a more prospective character as they remind the children and their families that a new phase in the children's lives is about to begin. In fact, a mixture of the past, present, and future were apparent in community-wide events like the children's singing performance in their last year of preschool and the sports day for fifth graders a few weeks before they finished their time in elementary school. Both events place children who are at a transition point in their lives in the spotlight in elaborately planned and widely attended community events. In the process the achievements of completing preschool and elementary school are highlighted because that is what qualifies the children for the attention they receive. The fun and joy of these events are deeply felt in the present as the events unfold. However, with the completion of the events, the children recognize that they will now collectively soon begin new phases in their lives.

These events are also important because while they center around certain children, they are open to the whole community. Thus whole families—parents, older and younger siblings, grandparents, and other relatives—attend to observe and often to record the activities in still pictures and video recordings. In these observations and later in shared reconstruction of the activities through the various recordings, different family and community members bring and take various things from these elements of civic society.

For organizers of the events, there is a civic pride in celebrating the lives of the children of the community in such a public and communal way. For adult members of the family, there is the positive recognition that their child or grandchild is becoming a more active member of the community and is growing up. For younger siblings there is not only fun and entertainment in witnessing the event, but also an anticipation of the future when they will have their turn in the spotlight.

Life Course Theory

Finally, our findings and interpretations can be related to elements of life course theory, most especially in terms of Entwisle and Alexander's (1999) notions of the role of social and psychological capital of parents for their children's academic achievement and status attainment. In their work in the United States, Entwisle and Alexander point out that wealthy parents, given their greater economic resources and greater access to better funded schools, have greater economic and social capital than parents of working class and poor children. Despite these differences, however, elementary school can be somewhat of an equalizer since many poor children, like the children of the wealthy, make educational gains during the first years of schooling. However, Entwisle and Alexander found in their research that poor children fall behind in the summer because their parents lack the psychological capital (parenting styles that promote intellectual curiosity and cognitive growth) that middle- and upper-class parents possess.

Although there were some differences in economic resources across the families of the children we studied in Modena, both social and psychological capital seemed to play much less of a role in all the early educational achievements of the children, compared to the United States. First, regarding economic and social capital, preschool education is universal and fully government supported in Italy. In addition, elementary education is federally funded and economic resources for schooling do not vary across communities and regions of the country. This does not mean that all regions are equal, as quality of teachers can vary even though their basic training and salaries may be the same.

Second, regarding psychological capital, the high quality of preschool programs with intensive parental involvement is important. Here our data allows us to speak of the parents of only two schools in Modena, but we believe these schools are representative of preschools and elementary schools in the city. It was clear in our findings that all children and their parents were well prepared for first grade from the participation in a wide range of priming events in the 3 years of preschool. We also found from interviews with children, parents, and teachers that during summers and over the 5 years of elementary school that interactions in families often promoted and supplemented educational processes in the schools. Although parents had to adjust to the fact that they could not enter the elementary classroom at the beginning and end of the school day as they did in preschool, over time they found they had ample time to meet with teachers. They also found that as in the preschool they could take on major roles in the planning of end-of-the-year parties and activities. In sum, the parents felt that they understood and were expected to play a part in their children's educational activities given the strong tradition of family involvement that was established in preschool.

In this sense the psychological capital of the Modenese parents was something promoted in the organization and structure of the community's early education system. Further, as we touched on earlier, we discovered in interviews and observations that older siblings and the older siblings of friends provided psychological capital for many of the children. Older siblings served as models for what was expected in regard to the changing nature of educational demands first in elementary school and then in preschool. Parents reported that older siblings were important in introducing the younger children to the structure of the new educational system and changes in educational activities (such as homework, the introduction of math, the multiple teachers and classes in middle school, and so on).

Our data do not allow us to make the argument that there was no variation in psychological capital across the families. There probably existed some variation in parenting styles to promote the growth of literacy and cognitive skills across families. In our interviews some parents reported working with their children on homework and planning educational activities in the summer more than other parents. However, all parents reported engaging in such activities. We believe that this psychological capital can be related to the social class and educational attainment of parents themselves, as in the United States. On the other hand, unlike in the United States, there is a promotion of parental psychological capital in the curriculum and goals of the government-supported preschool and elementary school through rich traditions of parental involvement in these institutions. Once the children reached middle school, such parental involvement lessened. However, the experiences of parents in preschool and elementary school contributed to their confidence in supporting their children's educational progress and achievement at this level as well.

IMPLICATIONS FOR EARLY EDUCATION IN ITALY

Our findings have a number of implications for current early education policies in Italy as well as for new policies that are now under consideration and nearing implementation. Our study is especially important because while there have been numerous studies of the preschool system in Italy, little is known about children's transition to elementary school and the importance of the preschool experience for that transition.

Educational Practices

One major implication for educational practices that arose from our ethnographic study is the importance of priming events to help children during transitions. We have described many priming events that took place at the end of preschool, during elementary school, and again toward the end of elementary school. All these events, and especially those preceding transitions to new schools, are very important not only because they help children adjust to new settings and demands, but also because they are moments that involve the participation of children, families, teachers, and the larger community. For this reason we can state that priming events develop at multiple planes of analysis, involving individuals, interpersonal relations, and the whole community.

However, when we interviewed preschool and elementary school teachers, as well as parents, most of them did not think of such events as priming. We had to explain what we meant by priming events, and still many teachers reported that they did not plan any priming event, even after we observed, for example, the visit to the school, which was undoubtedly a priming event. One of the implications of our study for Italian early education practices is therefore to emphasize the importance of priming events, stressing that the sequence of such events (discussing them before and after their performance) significantly contributes to the collective sharing of experiences that gives children the sense of participation and mutual sharing.

Another point of our study that has implications for actual practices in preschool is related to the growing interest in abilities concerning the development of literacy. All preschool teachers know that children are not expected to learn how to read and write before they finish preschool, and therefore all the activities they organize around literacy (reading together, asking individual children to perform collective reading, assigning homework related to long-term projects, and so on) are not meant to actually teach them to read and write but as prerequisites for these skills. During the observations we carried out in preschool, however, we came to realize that these activities are actually important for much more than just developing cognitive prerequisites, because they serve as ways to familiarize children with topics that will become daily activities in elementary school, and also give an answer to the pressing interest children manifest about literacy. It is not surprising, then, that children gradually incorporated activities about literacy into their own peer culture in peer activities. They also, as we have documented in their recordings in Bill's notebook, displayed literacy skills that became progressively richer and richer. In the last 6 weeks of preschool Bill's notebook was filled with words and phrases produced by the majority of children.

A final implication for early education practices in preschool and elementary school concerns the links between school and peer culture. We have discussed how school and peer cultures converge and share many commonalities in preschool, while the gap between the two becomes more evident in elementary school. A consideration of the meanings of peer culture for the transition is an important issue that needs to be dealt with by preschool and elementary school teachers, because when the school and peer culture are integrated, children develop a stronger interest and attachment to school. We believe this integration would be greater if the composition of the classes in elementary schools took into account which preschool the children attended, at least in terms of number and gender of children. Earlier we discussed the problems that one boy, Renato, experienced during the transition to elementary school. His problems were mainly related to the structure of the group in terms of peer culture. Although he made the transition to his new class with some other children from the Giuseppe Verdi preschool, they were all girls. Moreover, in the new class there were few boys, most of whom came together from another preschool and formed a clique that resisted Renato's attempts to enter. It will be helpful for teachers who are called upon to divide the children entering elementary school into class groups to take into account children's peer culture, which can have a great influence on allowing a smooth transition to the new system.

Systemwide Reforms

Our study was carried out in the period 1996–2002. In 2003, a reform of the educational system was proposed by the Ministry of Education, concerning many aspects of the whole school system from preschool to university. By the end of 2004, only a few changes have received full implementation in the schools, and some of these concern aspects not addressed by our study (e.g., the contents of the curriculum of history). We briefly consider here only those aspects of the reform that are relevant to the discussion we present in this book.

As we noted in Chapter 1, at the time we collected the data for our study children entered *scuola dell'infanzia* in their fourth year of life (they had to be 3 years old before December 31) and remained in the same school for 3 years. In 2003 the rules changed: Children can enter preschool and elementary school one year earlier. Parents decide if they want their children (only those who were born in the first months of the year) to be enrolled one year earlier or at the "traditional" age, and their decision cannot be refused. Moreover, a child who enters preschool one year earlier does not have to leave it one year earlier: One child may enter preschool when he is 3 and leave it when he is 5, while another child of the same age may leave preschool when he is 6.

This point has generated much debate, involving not only teachers and families, but the whole country. We will not enter into details about the practical problems that this aspect of the reform actually has to deal with, but rather we stress one point that in our opinion has not been given due consideration: the sudden interruption of the school and peer culture. When parents decide to enroll their child in elementary school one year earlier, this affects all the children in the group. Imagine that a group of 20 children (like the one we observed in its third year of preschool) all of a sudden breaks into two groups at the end of the second year, with some children leaving it and starting elementary school and some others remaining. This can have profound consequences on the whole planning of the year's activities, and it especially does not contribute to the communal construction of priming events and emotional bonds that are important moments preceding transitions.

The second aspect of the reform concerns a change in the length of the school day and total number of hours per week children attend elementary school, and can be summed up in the reduction of school hours. The main idea is that children will have school only in the mornings, 6 days a week as compared to full-day programs 5 days a week (with 4 hours of classes in the morning, then 2 more hours of classes after a 2 hour lunch break). Those children whose parents work and who need to remain in school in the afternoon will do other activities, or homework under the new system. This change, like the previous one, has been very much debated. For its highly political character, it has been attacked much more, and the result is that the situation is now very different in the various regions. In most parts of Emilia-Romagna, the school directors have so far found ways to "escape" this change, and therefore schools at the end of 2004 are still full-time. It is not clear, how long this ability to avoid implementation of the new legislation can continue.

If the full-time schools become morning schools for all children and afternoon schools only for children who need all-day care, it is clear that the whole organization will dramatically change. Of relevance to our study, children will have less time to share within the peer culture because recess will only be 10 minutes in the morning; lunch and siesta periods, during which children are now involved in free play and spend time with friends, will not be the same for the whole group. Again, what will be limited in this way is the opportunity to create bonds and establish a strong peer culture, which is a central point of the children's lives as shown in our longitudinal study.

A third point in the reform is the number and role of teachers in elementary school. Our study was carried out in a situation where two teachers were equally responsible for one class. As a general feature of Italian schools, the same two teachers remained with the same class for 5 years, while for practical reasons the classes we observed had a number of math teachers changing over the 5-year cycle. In any case, the structure of all classes remained predictable, with the math teachers nominated each year.

The change regarding teachers is that one teacher will be considered the main teacher of the class, while several other teachers will be teaching specialized subjects or will carry out specific projects. It is not completely clear so far how this change will be handled by the schools, and it is not yet implemented in the schools in Modena. The changes would have consequences in the continuity we experienced while making the transition with the children during our study. The situation we observed in elementary school was very similar in terms of structure to that of the preschool, and this is one of the things that made the children's transition very smooth.

Of course, we cannot anticipate how these three major changes will actually affect the lives of children, families, and teachers, and so far they have only partially been implemented. One of the interesting directions for future research will be to study the effects of any changes that are indeed implemented, and to discuss the impact they have on children's lives and schooling.

CONCLUSION

Our study provides just a beginning for studying children's early life transitions during the period of early education. Although we have a sample of only one preschool and one elementary school in Modena, Italy, our observations of these two schools were intensive, long-term, and highly detailed. We have learned a great deal about the children's transition from preschool to elementary school and their elementary school experience as well as their transition to middle school. These schools and children are representative of other schools and children in Modena and, we believe, in the Emilia-Romagna area of Italy more generally. The detailed knowledge our longitudinal study provides about schools in this area is important given its reputation as having some of the highest quality early education in the world. A lot is known about preschools in the Emilia-Romagna region, but less about the transition to and quality of education in elementary school. Our study helps provide needed knowledge in this area.

Future studies of early education in other parts of Italy, especially the South, would be very useful for building on our work. We hope our study will spur researchers in Italy to undertake such work, and we are working with colleagues to develop such studies in the future.

CHAPTER 12

Drawing Implications for Fundamental Change in American Early Education

Despite the fact that our research involved a small ethnographic case study, its longitudinal design and fit with other work on early education in Reggio Emilia do allow us to consider its implications for early education policy and programs in the United States. We start by considering some more specific implications in line with what we see as middle-range policy initiatives in the United States that could build on the most positive features of the preschool and elementary school programs in Modena. Here policy shifts involving major changes in educational institutional structure as well as large economic expenditures would not be necessary. We then go on to discuss some of the major differences between the Italian and American systems and our recommendations for more fundamental changes in American early education in line with our findings.

SOME SPECIFIC IMPLICATIONS AND RECOMMENDATIONS

Many of our findings are similar to earlier work on Reggio Emilia, which has described the most positive features of that preschool program, suggested applied implications, and carried out such applied programs mainly in various private preschools in the United States (Cadwell, 1997, 2003; Edwards, Gandini, & Forman, 1998; Giudici, Rinaldi, & Krechevsky, 2001). Our work shows that what we know about Reggio Emilia can be generalized to Modena and that features of both systems can be important in Italian children's transition to first grade. Our work adds to this earlier work in that we actually studied transitions to and in an Italian elementary school as well as preschool. Given these additional findings, we argue that many of the positive aspects of the preschool curriculum are relevant not just to American preschools (including government-supported programs like Head Start), but also to

American kindergartens, which serve children of the same age as the children in their final year of preschool in Modena.

We believe that specific activities that enriched children's educational experiences and social lives in the Modena preschool also served as important priming events for their transition to first grade. Here we want to highlight some of these activities and suggest that they could be implemented in many private preschools, Head Start, and public kindergartens in the United States.

Integration of Art and Literacy

American schools could develop an orientation to reading and writing by building on young children's interest and skills in visual and graphic language. As Katz (1998) notes, in preschools and kindergartens in the United States these skills are often promoted as part of art education and instruction. Seldom are such skills integral parts of long-term projects like the ones on "light and dark" and the "Wizard of Oz" that we documented in our findings in the Modena preschool. In fact, long-term projects in general are not common in American preschools and kindergartens, and we would suggest they should be (see Helm & Katz, 2001; also see O'Mara-Thieman, 2003, for an example of such a project in a American combined kindergarten and first-grade classroom). At the very least the introduction of children to reading and writing can be integrated with children's artwork and skills in the production of graphic language.

Group Discussion

In both the Modena preschool and elementary school, meeting times were devoted to talking with children as a group rather than to individual children or having each individual child taking a turn to talk. In fact, debate and discussion were highly valued. Every child came to realize that the stating of specific opinions was their right, and they claimed this right by often stating, "I have something to say!" or *Secondo me* ("In my opinion"). Such discussion demands a tolerance for what looks like disorder to many American adults: children interrupting each other and even the teachers; children moving from their seats to make a point or more closely inspect an object, picture, or book under discussion; and a general increase in the volume of talk and discussion. We found, however, that there was clear excitement and learning in these free-spirited debates, as well as a sense of community. Besides, order was easily restored when the children went beyond established limits. Additionally, such discussion demands a different orientation to time. Allowing for extensive discussion may mean the reading of a certain book or a phase of a long-term project may be carried over to the next day or even later. However, once teachers move away from rigid schedules that stress getting things done over greater participation and learning, they discover that time can be stretched and not forced into preestablished units or frames.

Field Trips

Frequent field trips to museums, monuments, gardens and parks, plays and performances, and workplaces were central to the curriculum in the Modena preschool. Such trips are not only educational, but highly enjoyable for children. Perhaps even more important, they break down age segregation as children get out into the community and interact with adults of varying ages. As we saw in our findings, these field trips always involved initial discussion, the taking and experiencing of the trip, and a reconstruction of the event in discussion and artwork. In fact, the rooms of the school and the children's portfolios were full of artwork and pictures based on field trips.

In the United States such field trips are a positive staple of many Head Start programs because the buses used to bring the children to the centers are available to take them on field trips. In Modena the parents who could afford it paid small fees for the bus and driver for field trips for all children. Such fees would be affordable in many American private preschools, and buses could be available in kindergarten, although schools might have to depend on drivers to volunteer or pay them for the extra service.

Introduction to Foreign Language

In the Modena preschools the children began formal instruction in a foreign language at age 4 and the time for lessons was extended at age 5. This instruction in English occurred in all the schools in the city and provided the children with a general introduction to the language. Like all language instruction, it also introduced students to different cultures and customs as the learning of songs, rhymes, and short stories were key aspects of lesson plans. In Modena this introduction was also important because the children would begin formal instruction in English in the third grade of elementary school. Thus they had a familiarity with the language and a foundation on which to build. In American schools instruction in foreign language often does not begin until middle school even though most experts feel that beginning at an early age would be optimal.

In American private preschools, Head Start programs, and kindergartens a general introduction to a foreign language (especially Spanish) would be highly beneficial. Here schools may be able to depend on volunteers if finances were not available. In any case, given the ethnic diversity of American students and the large increase in the Spanish-speaking population, early exposure to and use of Spanish by young children would be culturally enriching.

Parental Involvement

In the Modena preschool, parental involvement is high for a host of interrelated reasons. First, children stay together with the same teachers for all 3 years of preschool and parents get to know the teachers, children, and each other well. Also, as is well known from studies of Reggio Emilia schools, the documentation of projects, trips, and other activities serve as memory traces allowing parents to enter the school and literally see, touch, and read documents, displays, and artwork that capture their children's education. Further, parents are asked to participate in weekend homework assignments (especially in the final year of preschool) and keep records of educational activities they engage in with their children over the summer months in the children's individual portfolios. Finally, there are frequent teacher-parent meetings, and each class has a parental governing council that plans school trips, takes up collections for needed school resources, and organizes end-of-the-year parties.

American preschools and kindergartens have varying degrees of parental involvement, but few approach what we found in Modena and what has been reported in studies of schools in Reggio Emilia. One reason is that American parents have fewer opportunities to get to know each other, as teachers and even the makeup of classes change from year to year. In Modena, meetings with parents are part of paid work hours for teachers and are taken seriously by all parents and not just parents whose children have special needs or who are experiencing behavioral or academic problems. In the United States, variation by class and subcultural groups exists in work schedules, free time, and available transportation and work against parental involvement. Nonetheless, one of the most positive features of the Modena preschool and elementary school we studied was high parental involvement. Parental involvement is often a key positive feature of Head Start programs and is an important feature in some private preschools. However, it is fair to say that there is little research to show that parental participation is a mainstay of American kindergartens. American schools must find ways to increase parental participation especially in the important kindergarten and early years of elementary school. Above all, parents must feel more at home in their children's schools than they do at present.

Civic Engagement

A final specific implication of our findings for American preschools and kindergartens relates to the importance of civic community and engagement.

We have discussed at some length our findings of civic events that involve or center around children, such as particular holidays like Carnevale. Also in Modena we saw the complex organization, preparation, and enjoyment of civic events that specifically celebrated the lives of children who were finishing preschool and elementary school. These traditions are a reflection of civic community in Italy more generally, which can be traced back to the early Middle Ages (Putnam, 1993). However, their importance for the quality of life and socialization of children have remained relatively unexplored. In the United States, civic traditions exist in many of our cities, rural communities, and small towns. Children are often participants, and in some cases the event may be especially for children; but we know very little about the existence of traditions that mark children's transitions and their evolving membership in their culture. The planning and integration of such events around early schooling and life transitions would add much to American childhood and their experiences in early education.

IMPLICATIONS FOR FUNDAMENTAL CHANGE

So far we have discussed implications of our research that could be integrated into the present system of preschool and elementary education in the United States. Others would require more fundamental change.

Expansion of Early Education

A key feature of the Italian system is universal full-day preschool education for 3–5-year-olds. Although preschool is not mandatory in Italy, over 96 percent of 3–5-year-olds attend full-day programs throughout the country, and attendance is 100 percent in Modena. The United States has a very limited preschool program at the federal level for 3- and 4-year-olds, while kindergarten for 5-year-olds is offered by individual states as part of elementary school.

In the Untied States the Head Start program for economically disadvantaged children provides mainly half-day programs for 4- and some 3-year-olds. Head Start is seen as a compensatory or intervention program for poor children who are believed to be less prepared to enter kindergarten than other American children. Head Start has been extended in coverage several times since its inception in the 1960s. In the federal budget for the fiscal year 2005, $6.94 billion has been allocated for Head Start. This amounts to a very modest increase of around $270 million from the previous year and barely keeps up with inflation (U.S. Office of Management and Budget, 2005). The increase is particularly small considering that the new Head Start Act has a number of new initiatives. First, there is a mandate that 50 percent of Head Start teachers have B.A. degrees by 2008, but there are no extra funds to increase pay to attract those with higher education. Second, an initiative by President Bush requires that all 4-year-old participants in Head Start be tested in math, literacy, and language. No additional funds have been provided for the testing, and many experts in early education dispute the need for such tests. There is a fear that these new requirements without needed increases in the Head Start budget may divert funds away from health screening, nutrition evaluations, social services, and parental involvement. In short, under the present Republican administration in the White House and majority in Congress, Head Start seems to be moving in the wrong direction.

Beyond Head Start other subsidies go to provide child care for poor children at the state level through Title XX of the Social Security Act at the discretion of individual states. Finally, the federal government provides the "dependent care tax credit" on federal income taxes that gives some benefits to the middle and upper classes to help with private child care and early education costs. Most working-class and poor parents do not benefit from this tax credit because they pay little or no income tax, but do pay federal payroll taxes and other taxes at the state level.

The United States is far behind Italy in providing early education programs for 3- and 4-year-olds. Therefore, most families are responsible for finding their own child care or early education in an open market system. Numerous studies have found private child care and early education in the market system to be poor to mediocre in quality, while it is a major expense in terms of percentage of overall income for many families except the upper middle classes and the wealthy (Blau & Mocan, 2002; Brauner, Gordic, & Zigler, 2004; Helburn & Bergmann, 2002).

Kindergarten programs for 5-year-olds vary widely across the states with about 55 percent of states offering full-day programs, while the rest have only half-day programs. There is wide variation in the age set for entrance into kindergarten, and in a number of states attendance is not mandatory. Attendance varies from a low of 53 percent to a high of 100 percent with the overwhelming majority of states having at least 80 percent attendance rates (Vecchiotti, 2003). A few states now offer or have initiatives to offer universal preschool for 4-year-olds (see Gormley & Phillips, 2003; Raden, 1999; Vecchiotti, 2003).

This brief review reveals that the United States lags far behind Italy in terms of early education programs to enrich children's intellectual, social, and cultural experiences and to prepare children for transition to first grade. Furthermore, the weak and poorly integrated programs in the United States fail to support single parent families and families in which both parents work (especially those in the working-class) who are in dire need of quality child care.

These differences are due to variation in cultural values in the United States and Italy regarding family rights and responsibility and government programs designed to support families in the care and education of their young children. In terms of values and attitudes about child care and early education, it is noteworthy that the American government has awarded millions of dollars in grant money to assess the possible negative effects of nonmaternal child care and early education in the preschool years. For example, a recent study by the National Institute of Child Health and Human Development (NICHD) Early Child Care Research Network (2003) found that the longer the time preschool children spent in nonmaternal child care (regardless of type of care), the more externalizing problems and conflict children displayed later at home and in kindergarten as reported by parents and teachers.

These findings are difficult to interpret: The findings were statistically significant but barely so; trained observers of the same children in kindergartens did not observe the significant problem behaviors and conflict the teachers did; and it is impossible to determine if the findings reported by parents and teachers are related to children having spent time in nonmaternal care at a very young age or just having spent longer periods of time in such care. The issue about age at first care is important because in Italy (and nearly all European countries) there are long periods of paid maternity leave, while such paid leave is not provided in the United States (Kamerman, 2000). Thus the negative findings could be the result of the failure of the United States to provide paid maternity leave for parents during their child's first year of life.

In any case, studies like the NICHD one, their support by extensive funding from the federal government, and the attention they receive in the American press have no counterparts in Italy. In fact, rather than seeing such nonmaternal care as a social problem that the government must spend money to study, Italy provides funding for federal programs to allow working mothers to stay at home with children during the first months, quality child care programs when mothers return to work for children from 18 months to 3 years of age, and early education for all 3–5-year-olds.

However, the differences of investments in families and the quality of life of young children in the two countries go beyond cultural values. Values are only one part of the equation of early education in Italy and the United States. Variations in the outcomes of political struggles and power relations that affect the development of various social welfare policies in the two countries are also important (see Corsaro & Emiliani, 1992). In the United States the conservative, Republican control of the Congress for many of the last 40 years as well as frequent Republican control of the executive branch has worked against the development of social welfare programs affecting young children, such as paid maternity leave, child care, and early childhood education. In Italy the strength of unions, coalition governments of the center right and left, and to some extent the power of the Catholic Church all played a role in the development and implementation of legislation that established extensive federal welfare programs providing family leave, child care, and early childhood education (Corsaro & Emiliani, 1992; Della Sala, 2002; Gandini & Edwards, 2001; Pistillo, 1989).

As a result Italy has in place an extensive and coordinated set of programs that invest in young children, while the United States does not. In difficult economic periods in Italy, programs for children, like all social programs, are reevaluated and may have levels of funding cut. However, the programs for families and children have not been seriously challenged and have in many cases been expanded. In contrast, in the United States economic recessions and a general aversion to raising taxes by the majority of Americans have made it difficult to garner political support for new programs even when there is substantial public demand for such programs (Brauner, Gordic, & Zigler, 2004).

Given variations in cultural values as well as the reality of differences in the political-economic system and power structures in Italy and the United States, it is unrealistic that anything like Italy's universal preschool program or its direct federal funding of elementary schools will be easily established in the United States. Nonetheless, there are some present initiatives and proposals in the United States that could move us closer to the Italian system.

First, as we noted earlier, some states (Georgia and Oklahoma) now offer universal preschool education for all four year olds (Gormley & Phillips, 2003; Raden, 1999; and Vecchiotti, 2003). Similar initiatives have also been proposed in New York and California. Funding for these programs varies from using lottery revenues to general state tax receipts. The success of such programs can serve as models for similar initiatives in other states. However, what is really needed is for the federal government to supplement state funds for such programs with block grants. So far the federal government has become less involved in early education even in Title XX funding. Furthermore, it is extremely doubtful that money earmarked for further testing of children will be used to support states in developing early education not only for 4-year-olds but also 3-year-olds.

A second possibility would be a major expansion of the Head Start program. Head Start has generally been a half-day compensatory program for 4-year-olds from very poor families to help children prepare for kindergarten. The program was expanded somewhat in line with changes in welfare policies that demanded mothers receiving welfare move to work within a 2-year period. Thus, more child care was needed, and some Head Start programs were expanded to include 3-year-olds and provide full-day care and early education. However, as we discussed earlier, funding for Head Start in fiscal year 2005 barely keeps up with inflation, while adding new requirements for testing and training for teachers.

In fact, a wider and substantial overhaul of Head Start would be necessary to truly address the problem of child care and early education of poor and working-class children. Not only should all 3- and 4-year-olds be covered in all-day programs, but the income restriction should be raised to include all of the working poor in the United States as well as those who are poor and cannot find work or are in need of job training. Such a change in the Head Start system would also demand better training and pay for teachers and other staff. The recent new requirement that 50 percent of Head Start teachers have B.A. degrees by 2008 is a step in the right direction. However, not providing funds to increase pay to attract better trained teachers means that this mandate is unlikely to be met. Furthermore, given present rates of pay for Head Start teachers, we can only expect high rates of turnover for teachers with better training as they will look to better paying jobs in elementary schools.

The two proposals above would clearly face difficulties in gaining substantial public support as well as funding at the state or federal level. Another change that would bring the American system into at least some compatibility with Italy would be full-day kindergarten in all states. Numerous studies have detailed the positive effects of full-day kindergarten for children's social, emotional, and cognitive development as well as for their transition to first grade (see Vecchiotti, 2003, for a review). There is also widespread public support for full-day kindergarten.

However, full-day kindergarten programs demand more funds for teachers, materials, and physical space and buildings. In many states with only half-day programs there may be support for the concept, but actual implementation is often a low funding priority. Additionally, there is usually resistance for increased taxation to fund the expansion of kindergarten. Here again some federal subsidies to states with full-day programs may speed up a process that is moving in the right direction, but still seems a number a years away from full implementation. This is especially true given the Bush administration's focus on testing in the limited funding from the No Child Left Behind Act.

Improvement of the Elementary School Experience

Our results and the Italian experience in general point to other possibilities for program change or further development of existing programs at the elementary school level. We found that a major positive feature of Italian preschools and elementary schools was the structure of keeping groups of children together with the same teachers throughout the education process. This structure led to supportive teacher-student relations, integrations of school and peer cultures, and substantial levels of parental involvement. We also found that the existence of the organizational structure in both preschool and elementary school positively supported the children's transition and adaptation to elementary school.

In the United States, the practice of having teachers stay with the same group of students over all years of preschool or elementary school is to our knowledge very rare or nonexistent. In private preschools and Head Start programs that have multiple age groups, children normally stay together unless there is a transfer to a different school. Rarely, however, do these groups have the same teachers over the course of 2 years or more. If both children and teachers stayed together throughout preschool there would be closer connection and support between the school and peer cultures, or what Maccoby and Lewis (2003) refer to as "stronger attachment" of children to their preschool and preschool teachers.

In elementary schools in the United States there has been experimentation with age grouping (mixing children of one to three age groups together with one or two teachers) and looping. *Looping* involves having children stay with teachers for more than the typical 1-year time period (usually 2–3 years). Looping better fits the Italian model. These practices are rare in the United States and initiating such models would, of course, be extra work for teachers making the change from the typical pattern. Yet, in cases where multiage grouping and looping have occurred, studies report positive reactions of children, teachers, and parents (Graue, 1999; Jacobson, 1997); but there has been little research on multiage grouping or looping regarding student academic achievement and other student outcomes. As Graue points out regarding looping, we know conceptually why it is implemented and what values and practices it tends to endorse, "but knowledge of its efficacy, or even of the range of is implementation, is still quite underdeveloped" (p. 114).

Given our results in this research, we would be surprised to find that looping would have negative effects on educational processes in elementary schools in the United States. In fact, we would predict that it would lead to better integration of school and peer culture within classrooms and develop a stronger attachment to school among the children. We encourage studies to determine its effectiveness, but more important, we argue for a wide range of implementation to provide a broader number of cases for such evaluation studies. Also given our findings, we argue that a quick dismissal of looping if it shows no long-term advantage would be premature. There are many positive effects of keeping children and teachers together including bonding between teachers and students and among students, attachment and commitment to school, ability to allow children to progress at different paces, and stronger parental involvement.

THE FUTURE OF PROGRESSIVE EARLY EDUCATION IN THE UNITED STATES

We hope that this study can stimulate educational researchers and policy makers in the United States to work toward the development and implementation of a more coherent, equitable, and enriching early education system for all American children. While some developments in certain states encourage us to believe that this is not a vain hope, we can have little optimism at the federal level. The reelection of George W. Bush as president along with a Republican Congress make any possibility of increased investment in early education highly unlikely in the short term.

The ongoing involvement of American troops in Iraq, an increasing federal debt, a developing crisis in health care (Medicare and Medicaid) and Social Security, all work against any expectations that the present administration is serious about investing in America's children. In a country where over 16 percent of children live in poverty and 12 percent of children are without health care, it is perhaps unreasonable to expect much investment in early education. Yet a country that ignores its children, does so at its own peril. Changes in socioeconomic values and political power can be cyclical, and a movement toward more progressive social policies for young children may occur in the not too distant future. If it does, educators should be ready to act and put to use this information about quality early childhood education as practiced in Italy and much of Western Europe.

The School System in Italy and in the City of Modena

Preschool children in Italy have the possibility of attending two different types of preschool services. The *asilo nido* (early day care) takes children from 4 months old until they turn 3 years old, and the *scuola dell'infanzia* (preschool) is for the care and education of children from 3 to 5 years old. Although we use the term *scuola dell'infanzia* throughout this appendix, it has only recently replaced the term *scuola materna* ("maternal school"), reflecting the change in the philosophy of preschools from a custodial aim to an educational one. Neither the *asilo nido* nor the *scuola dell'infanzia* is compulsory. Quite a low percentage of Italian children attend *asilo nido* (about 8 percent, as reported in the 2002 national statistics), but this percentage is much higher in Modena (38 percent in 2002), which has always been a very progressive city regarding preschool education. Attendance in the *scuola dell'infanzia* is nearly universal. Over 96 percent of all Italian children attended in 1996, but the attendance in Emilia-Romagna reached 100 percent.

The primary and secondary school systems are organized on three levels. Children start the first level, *scuola elementare* (elementary school), when they are 6 years old, and they attend the same school for 5 years. Children next attend a 3-year *scuola media* (middle school), and then a 5-year *scuola superiore* (high school) before they can enter the university. Elementary school, middle school, and the first 2 years of high school (until children turn 16) are compulsory (see Figure A.1).

All the different types of schools are organized in ways that guarantee a certain degree of stability and continuity for the children and teachers. Children can enter the *asilo nido* in the first, second, or third year of life (4 months to 2 years old), but once they have entered it, they will stay with the same group of children and teachers until their last term. The group is much smaller (10 to 12 children) in the first year as these children need more care and

Figure A.1. The Structure of the Italian School System

Level	Ages	Attendance
Asilo nido	Ages 4 months to 2 years old	Noncompulsory
Scuola dell'infanzia	3 to 5 years old	Noncompulsory
Scuola elementare	6 to 10 years old	Compulsory
Scuola media	11 to 13 years old	Compulsory
Scuola superiore	14 to 18 years old	Compulsory to Age 16

attention than the older children; the group grows to around 20 children in the second and third years with two to three teachers for each class (see Gandini & Edwards, 2001, for a detailed discussion of infant and toddler care in Italy).

Even more stability is guaranteed in the *scuola dell'infanzia*. A large majority of children start when they are 3 years old, and the whole group of children and teachers stay together for 3 years. Changes in the group (a child or teacher leaving, others entering) during this 3-year period are rare, as there is much less geographical mobility in Italy compared to the United States. Parents can keep their children in the same school after a move, but they would need to provide transportation as there is no bus service.

The same stability is true for the elementary school level. Every class attending elementary school has two to three teachers, and they stay together for 5 years. Grouping of children is decided on by the first-grade teachers in consultation with the teachers from the *scuola dell'infanzia*. The main criteria are gender composition and placement of children with special needs. Parents are not consulted in these initial groupings. In middle schools and high schools, every class has eight or more teachers representing the specialized subjects of instruction in the higher grades of schools, but the group of children remains stable throughout each school level.

Each level of the school system can be public or private. Although it is difficult to make general statements about the nature of private schools because of the very different characteristics of private schools in the various regions, a majority of children attend public schools, particularly on the elementary and middle school levels.

In the rest of this appendix, we describe in more detail the historical features, organizational aspects, and educational philosophies of the *scuola dell'infanzia* and the *scuola elementare*. We focus directly on Emilia-Romagna and in particular on the city of Modena (with a population of about 185,000), which is representative of the other cities in the region.

THE SCUOLA DELL'INFANZIA

The *scuole dell'infanzia* in Italy consist of four different types, two public and two private: state-run public schools city-run or communal public schools, private Catholic schools, and private cooperative schools organized by societies engaged in the field of social work. Public preschools are fully supported by the state or city government, but private schools also receive some local government support if they follow prescribed regulations for the quality of education. For example, they must have no more than 25 children per class, accept children with special needs, and guarantee the daily schedule, and their teachers must complete 20 hours per year of training organized by the city government. The local government provides around 12 percent of the total budget of the private Catholic schools, while it provides a much higher percentage—nearly 60 percent—for private cooperative schools.

In Modena, there are 38 public preschools (22 are communal and 12 are state) and 24 private schools (20 Catholic and 4 cooperative). The number of public schools in Modena (and in the whole region) is among the highest in Italy. The percentage of private schools (especially Catholic) compared to public schools is much higher in other regions, especially in southern Italy. Overall, in Modena in the year when we collected data in the *scuola dell'infanzia* (1995–96), 55.6 percent of the population aged 3 to 6 attended public schools (43.9 percent in the communal schools and 11.7 percent in the state schools), and 43.9 percent attended private schools, mainly Catholic (38.8 percent). The total number of children attending school was in that year 99.5 percent and is now slightly over 100 percent, because some immigrant children who are not official residents are accepted into the schools.

History

The history of the *scuola dell'infanzia* in Modena, and to some extent in the whole Emilia-Romagna region, is deeply rooted to the social and cultural context of the wider community. Before looking at the details of the specific situation of Modena, we will describe in general terms the overall history of the preschool system in Italy.

In March 1968, the Italian Parliament passed Law No. 444 which officially recognized the government's right to be directly involved in preschool education. Later amendments to the law set forth guidelines (*orientamenti*) for educational activities in state preschools.

Development of preschool education was clearly linked to social and economic trends in Italy. Italy underwent rapid industrialization in the 1950s and early 1960s. During this period, often referred to as the "Italian miracle" or "economic miracle," there was mass migration from the rural areas to the cities (and from the South to the North) as workers left agricultural work for jobs in heavy industry and manufacturing. These economic changes had a profound effect on the quality of life of Italians. While a parliamentary committee on poverty declared that one family in eight lived in "utter destitution" in the early 1950s, by the 1960s Italy "had attained an overall economic profile and standard of living comparable to that of advanced capitalist nations" (Hellman, 1987, p. 357). At the same time, Italy became much more of a consumer society with major increases in the ownership of cars, televisions, telephones, and other consumer goods. These changes had significant effects on the family, especially a clear trend from extended to nuclear family structure. These developments brought about a reconception of early childhood and a growing consensus regarding the need for preschool education.

Given the changes brought about by rapid industrialization, the political climate of the 1960s, and the progressive educational movements that existed in the North, the time was ripe for legislation for the institution of state nursery schools or *scuole dell'infanzia*. In 1962 a center-left government (a coalition of moderate and liberal parties) was formed which decided to take up an earlier legislative initiative for direct state involvement in preschool education. This proposal was the result of growing interest in educational experimentation by local governments, most especially in the left-wing areas of the North. In particular, striking progressive preschool educational developments occurred in the Emilia-Romagna area. In Bologna, the major city in the region, the number of city-controlled preschools doubled in the 1960s, spurred on by the writings of such educational philosophers as Bruno Ciari. Ciari believed that preschool education was a means of giving every child, regardless of background, "a common cultural foundation upon which to grow as a person and citizen" (Pistillo, 1989, p. 161). He also argued for the communal and social management of all educational life, with an active role for parents through assemblies and committees (Baldisserri, 1980). This progressive movement was also stimulated by similar developments at this time in other European countries, especially Germany and France (Mozère, 1984).

One cannot forget, however, the power of the Catholic Church and its alliance with the Christian Democratic Party that was in power at the time. The Church controlled virtually all of the preschools that were established before the 1950s, and strongly opposed any attempts at government control (Pistillo, 1989). During the years of the "economic miracle," the Church argued that social problems resulting from rapid industrialization would be best met by a further expansion of private schools under its direction. It is important to note here that the Church never disputed the need for preschool education (i.e., educational programs for children from 3 to 5 years old). In fact, the Church stressed the need for such institutions under its control, at first, primarily as a form of compensatory education for poor children, but later to meet more general socialization and educational functions that could not be adequately provided in the family because of social and economic changes in the country (Corsaro & Emiliani, 1992).

The history of *scuole dell'infanzia* in Modena begins before the passage of Law No. 444 in 1968. At the beginning of the 1960s, the city registered a rapid growth in women's labor, both outside the home in factories and inside the home as artisans, especially for the textile industry. Thus pressure on the local government to support child care increased dramatically. The local government invested in child care programs in Modena beginning in 1964, when two *scuole dell'infanzia* were opened. The local government did not have any funds for opening schools, but new investments were decided upon and made in line with the general policies of left-wing regions, which devoted much work to supporting social requests from the population. These first schools that were opened in 1964 were in areas of the city where mothers themselves marched with their children, asking for public schools and early education.

The highest number of communal schools in Modena was registered in the period from 1970 to 1980, when there were 33 preschools. Later some schools had to be closed because of security reasons (they were not built in line with later laws about physical safety of public buildings), and in the second half of the 1980s there was also a decline in the birthrate. Since 1990 there has been a new increase in parental requests for communal schools, due to the high number of immigrants and a slow increase in the birthrate.

Modena has been one of the most progressive cities in Italy not only for opening communal preschools, but also for teacher training and for the strong links between schools and families. The *istituti magistrali,* a secondary school specializing in education lasting 4 years, was established in the late 1970s, and constitutes the teachers training of most present-day preschool teachers throughout Italy. Also their first year of teaching is normally seen as a training period.

Before that time, teachers needed to have 3 years of secondary school to prepare for required competency tests as part of employment in the school system. In 1968, when state-supported preschools started, there were only seven public schools for teacher training for the competency tests in Italy; all the other schools for teacher training (nearly 200 in number) were run by the Catholic Church. One point of controversy between the local government of Modena and the Church's control of the majority of schools had to do with teacher training and government exclusion of males from preschool education, which the Catholic Church supported. The exclusion of males implied a custodial orientation with women providing security and emotional support to preschool children. Such an orientation was vigorously opposed by progressives who supported primary education rather than custodial programs. Beginning in 1968 the local government of Modena organized a specific program to train preschool teachers, who then went to one of the seven public schools to pass the final exam. In 1972 Modena was the first city to require two teachers in each preschool class, who were to spend at least 4 hours per day together in the same class. This requirement increased the quality of these schools in several ways. First, it reduced the student-teacher ratio so that individual children received more attention. Second, it encouraged cooperation between the two teachers to pool their various talents and experiences in designing innovative curriculum and school projects. The fruits of such cooperation increased when the two teachers worked together for 4 to 5 years or longer as many of the teachers did.

Recently, in 1998, there was a major change in state requirements for the training of preschool and elementary school teachers. Under the new law, preschool (as well as elementary school) teachers have to attend 4 years of training at the university level in educational sciences and pass a competency test before teaching. The first group of teachers trained under the new law have just recently begun their teaching careers in Italian schools.

The strong link between preschools and families in Modena (as in other parts of Italy) is guaranteed since 1968 by the organization in each school of the *consiglio di gestione*. This is a committee directly organized and run by parents, following a precise plan, which has among its aims to promote activities in the schools, to evaluate the educational activities, and to facilitate the relations between parents and teachers. The committee in each school meets three times a year and is composed of three parents for each class (elected by the parents every year), a teacher for each class, and one member of the support staff (the group of people who clean and serve food in the schools).

Structure and Organization

Scuole dell'infanzia normally operate 8–10 hours a day, 5 days a week. However, some schools (especially in the South) follow a 5-hour timetable and do not provide a midday meal. Most schools are open from early September until the end of June.

The data for this study were collected in a communal public school in Modena. Parents apply for entering a communal school in January–February of the year when their child is going to be 3 years old. The child is assigned to a list that follows an order depending on several criteria, the most important of which are the closeness of the home to the school and having another child in the same school or in a nearby elementary school. The family income does not constitute criteria for acceptance in *scuole dell'infanzia*. Children who are not accepted into the communal schools still have the possibility of choosing a state or a private school.

Communal schools accept no more than 25 children per class with two teachers. There can be exceptions in cases of extraordinary numbers of children applying for schools, so the number can reach 29 children with three teachers. Additional teachers are also guaranteed for classes where there is a child with special needs. In Modena, communal schools normally have three to four age-segregated classes. The student-teacher ratio is very low; in 1995–96 it was 11.7 children to 1 teacher.

In these schools, children arrive before 9:00 A.M. and stay until 4:00 P.M. If extended child care is needed and documented, the children can arrive as early as 7:30 A.M. and stay until 6 P.M. Children have three meals at school: breakfast at 9:00, lunch at noon (prepared by an outside cooperative and brought to the schools in special packages), and a snack at 3:30. Special meals for children who require them (vegetarian, without pork, or for particular intolerances) are guaranteed.

There is a good deal of variation in the activities in the *scuole dell'infanzia*. In general, the curriculum covers several fields: art, literature, science, math, logic, and physical activities. The children in each age group have 2 hours per week of music, with a specialized teacher; 4- and 5-year-olds also have English lessons (1 hour a week for 4-year-olds and 2 hours a week for 5-year-olds) conducted by native speakers of English. Moreover, numerous field trips take place each year, such as visiting museums, the cathedral, a theatre, or a farm.

In the 2000–2001 city government contributed about 500 Euro per month for each child attending preschool from subsidies provided by the federal government. A parent in the highest income level paid 95 Euro per month, which corresponded to the cost of the meals. There was a lower rate of 60 Euro per month for middle-income families, and low-income families do not pay any fees. The parents were also asked to pay 10 Euro per month to a special fund under the control of the *consiglio di gestione*; the committee of each school decides autonomously how to use this money, for example, to promote particular activities such as sports or music or to finance special projects.

Teachers earned about 1000 Euro per month (13 months per year counting the Christmas month bonus) after taxes in 2000–2001. They have all the benefits accorded to state employees in Italy (free health insurance, maternity leave, holidays, and pension). They work 35 hours a week, 30 of which are spent in the class, and 5 in other activities (meeting with parents, specific training courses, activities planning). Teacher turnover is very low. In Modena there are teachers who have worked in the communal schools for as long as 25 years. Teachers can change schools only in the year when they are starting with a new 3-year-old group. Teachers, like all state employees in Italy as result of a general labor contract, cannot lose their jobs or be laid off from work except for very serious violations in their work, not, for example, because of a reduction in the number of students.

Preschool teacher salaries are very similar to that of elementary school teachers, and they have the same benefits. Although it is hard to estimate the status or prestige of preschool teachers compared to other teachers, it is safe to say that it is similar to that of elementary school teachers, but is not as high as secondary school teachers. Preschool education is highly valued in Italy (especially in the North) compared to the United States: Nearly 96 percent of all Italian 3–5-year-olds participate in preschool programs and the Italian government supports almost all costs (except for meals) of preschool education, compared to minimal financial support for preschool programs in the United States.

Educational Philosophy

Several prominent educational theorists in Italy (Bertolini, 1984; Frabboni, 1984; Manini, 1984) trace the connection of present-day educational theory in Italy to the classic work of Owen, Froebel, Agassi, and Montessori, and then outline what can best be described as an ecological view of child development (Bronfenbrenner, 1979). In this view the *scuola dell'infanzia* is an important educational context for the social, affective, and cognitive development of the child, but it is not limited to intellectual development. Rather the *scuola dell'infanzia* is seen as a place of life for the child. Activities such as playing, eating, and working together are thought to be as important as individual intellectual tasks. This communal orientation is developed more fully by a national commission of educators set up to evaluate the *orientamenti* of 1968, which stresses the relationship of the *scuola dell'infanzia* with the family and community (*Rapporto*, 1989).

The educational philosophy of *scuole dell'infanzia* in Modena can be synthesised in several important points. First is the focus on the children. The main idea that guides the planning of educational work is that the children participate in their own learning. In the 1960s, the pioneering educator, Loris Malaguzzi became coordinator of the first *scuole dell'infanzia* in Modena and promoted the view that school was not a kind of "second family," and the teacher was not a "substitute mother." Rather he believed that the preschool is a place where children must have opportunities to learn about life. In the early 1960s Malaguzzi found schools that had few materials and little financial resources. So one of his first activities was to meet with families to gather resources (books and financial contributions) and to discuss ways to organize activities in the school. In this way, his first contribution brought the schools and families together to plan for the future of preschools. (See Mantovani, 1998, for a collection of papers presented in a conference organized in honour of Malaguzzi after his death.)

A second focus is on the social and cultural context. Among the most innovative ideas of the first schools developed in this area are the open boundaries of the school. Already in 1968 parents could enter the school, take their child into class each morning, talk to the teachers, bring and exchange material, and so on. This helped to create the strong bonds between families and schools that are evident in the creation of the *consiglio di gestione*, where parents give voice to their ideas, opinions, and values about the school. The collaboration between the school and the social context has remained alive to the present day, and is shown in the importance given not only to cognitive learning, but also to social, affective, and emotional development.

Third is a focus on training of the teachers. We have already mentioned the fact that teachers are in continuous training, attending at least 20 hours of training every year. In the 1980s, Sergio Neri (2001) started working on a project with the teachers in Modena based on the idea that they needed a specialization in one particular field (art, music, logic, and so on), and that through the exchange among teachers of experiences of specialization, the schools would gain in quality and interests. More than 20 years ago then, many different specialization courses were established. It is fair to say that some teachers are continuing to follow the same course, and have become exceptionally well trained in their various specialized fields that now constitute one of the interests in their lives even beyond their work. Anyone visiting a school can easily see impressive examples of art, literature, and natural science in displays and exhibits. In the specialized courses teachers not only learn a particular subject, like art, but they also learn how to teach it to the children, using a method that starts from the children's interests and arrives to a the point of especially high quality production of material and artifacts.

Finally, there is a focus on building a strong relationship between the schools and the community. Schools are open, not only to the families but to the larger community. Children and teachers can often be seen in the city, visiting exhibitions or museums or just running, playing, and drawing in a park. But what is more important, their activities and artifacts are highly valued by the community. Consider a recent example: In 2002, all the communal schools in Modena participated in a special project. They were asked to design and produce a model of a bench on which people at the bus stops could sit while waiting for their bus to arrive. Teachers collected hundreds of pages of discussions, ideas, and opinions about what the children thought was important in designing such a bench. The children offered many different suggestions: They wanted a bench for eating ice cream; they wanted a bench with pillows; they wanted a bench to be very comfortable; they wanted a bench that could accommodate many different persons, like a child, a tall grandfather, a large or heavy person, and so on. Then each class built a model of its most preferred bench, relying on used or recyclable materials. The city collected the various models and organized a public exhibition that displayed the benches from all the different schools, along with posters of the many discussions that were part of their creation. The exhibition was presented in one of the oldest buildings of the Modena and lasted 2 weeks. Finally, the city selected several models as finalists and a number of the models are now used at city bus stops.

THE *SCUOLA ELEMENTARE*

The *scuole elementari* in Italy are public (state schools supported by the federal government) or private (mostly Catholic). In different regions the proportion of children attending public or private schools varies; in Emilia-Romagna, when we started data collection in the 1997–98 academic year, 86.4 percent of the children attended public schools. This percentage however, is, higher than in other regions, especially in the South, where there are still many Catholic schools.

In Modena, there are 27 state elementary schools, divided into 8 *circoli didattici* (under the direction of one manager), and 5 Catholic schools. State schools are free, as are books and other educational materials. The buildings are provided by the city, and the city offers some services: meals for children from poor families transportation, and support staff. The expense for families who choose a private elementary school varies considerably, but in 2000–2001 the average tuition for private schools in Modena was about 160 Euro per child per month (not including the cost of the meals).

Children start elementary school in September when they are 6 years old, and stay in the school in the same group of children and teachers for 5 years. At the end of the fifth year, they have to pass an exam before starting middle school. Each class in elementary school has a maximum number of 25 children; classes that include children with special needs are limited to 20 children.

The normal schedule for elementary school children is 30 hours of lessons per week. This schedule can be fulfilled through two types of organization. In *scuole a tempo pieno* (full-time schools) children have 6 hours of lessons (4 in the morning and 2 in the afternoon) for 5 days a week, but also stay in the school for another 2 hours every day to have lunch and free time. In these schools there are two teachers per class. *Scuole a moduli* ("block" schools) have different organizations: in some cases the children have 3 long days in school (7 hours of lessons per day plus time for lunch) and two short ones (4½ hours), while in other cases schools divide the whole schedule over 6 days a week (Monday through Saturday) for 5 hours each. In these schools there are three teachers per class, and they teach in more than one class (they have "blocks" of hours in different classes). In Modena, 23 of the 27 state schools are full-time.

The data for our study were collected in a full-time state school. Before presenting a detailed description of the structure and organization of this type of school, we will briefly summarize the history of elementary schools in Italy, particularly in Modena.

History

Before 1971, elementary schools in Italy were organized on a 24 hours a week schedule (4 hours a day in the morning for 6 days a week). Each class was open to 30 children, with one teacher. Law No. 820 in 1971 offered opportunities for changes in the 24 hours a week schedule, through the organization of more activities in the school with the aim of enriching each child's training and providing more services for children with few opportunities for learning within their families.

During this period Modena was very active in establishing new projects in the schools. Full-time schools started in the early 1970s with "official teaching" in the mornings, run by state-employed teachers, and "compensatory teaching" in the afternoon, run by teachers employed by the city government, who worked to offer children with fewer opportunities the possibility of being helped with homework or engaging in other educational activities. The rapid growth of these early full-time schools in Modena paralleled the high demand for preschools, due to the increasing number of working women.

From 1971 until 1985, there was gradual movement toward full-time schools open all day long for all children. These schools in fact started as a kind of compensatory education in the afternoon, but gradually morning and afternoon teachers started to coordinate, and the difference between official teaching (for everybody) in the mornings and compensatory teaching (only for some children) in the afternoon gradually disappeared. In 1985 all the elementary schools were run completely—mornings and afternoons—by state-employed teachers. The communal teachers that used to teach in the afternoon gradually moved to other work. The majority of them prepared for compensatory tests and started working for the state; others started teaching in preschools, and still others opened new centers for education, funded by the city government, offering information to teachers, opening libraries specialized in educational fields, or working directly to help teachers of children with special needs. These centers are still open in Modena, and they constitute important resources for all teachers.

In Modena, as we noted earlier, 23 of 27 elementary schools are full-time. This situation is not only a reflection of the needs of working parents, it is also symbolic of the value given by the citizens to an education that not only prepares children academically or intellectually but also offers different projects and activities that are important for social and emotional development. The presence of many full-time schools in the city is made possible by the services that the city government offers to state schools, such as support staff to guarantee the serving of lunch at school.

On the national level, in 1974 a set of decrees, the *Decreti Delegati*, were passed. The decrees addressed a number of organizational functions (e.g., institution of governing bodies or school boards, norms regarding the legal attributes of administrators, teachers, other personnel, and experimentation and research) for the overall school system. These decrees are especially important because they gave rise to a larger participation in the school on the part of families who could then take part in and vote for a number of issues regarding the schools.

In 1985 a set of new official curriculum programs for elementary schools was instituted. These programs distinguish four curriculum areas of teaching: language (Italian), scientific (math and science), social studies (history and geography), and practical education (art, music, and sports). Since 1985 all elementary classes have a weekly schedule of 30 hours and have at least two teachers, who can choose an area of specialization. When two teachers work in the same class (as in full-time schools), they choose to teach Italian or math, and then also teach some disciplines of the other areas; when three teachers work in a class (as in "block" schools), they are each specialized in one of the three first areas and then teach one practical discipline. In the years after 1985, the Ministry of Education required new training of all teachers in these areas of specialization.

Two laws are also important for today's organization of elementary schools, both passed by the recent center-left government. First, Law No. 138 of 1995 (*Carta dei servizi*) establishes several principles that have to be followed by all the schools. The schools have to guarantee equal opportunities for education to all the children and encourage parents to monitor their children's educational progress and to participate, to some extent, in the life of the school. The schools also have to plan specific projects for children with special needs or with learning difficulties. After 1995, families could decide which school they want their child to attend, depending on the kind of services that each school provides to the students.

The second innovative law is Law No. 275, passed in 1999, which promotes school autonomy. Each group of schools (under the direction of one manager) now receives funds from the Ministry of Education, and can use this money with a wide range of flexibility. The percentage of flexibility is

15 percent: that is, out of every 100 hours of school time, 85 have to be dedicated to the curriculum and 15 can be organized for different projects or disciplines, such as theatre or computer sciences, decided autonomously by the schools. The most evident consequence of such a law is the specific options offered to each group of schools for their students and families. At the beginning of the school year, the schools decide on the projects they will offer and inform the families. Before choosing a school, the parents can ask for information on the kind of specific projects it offers.

Structure and Organization

In the full-time schools in Modena, like the one where we conducted our research, children have 30 hours of lessons per week, but most of them spend 40 hours at school each week. Children start school at 8:30 A.M. They have 4 hours of morning lessons with a short break for snack. Lunch and recess follow, from 12:30–2:30. Finally, there are 2 more hours of afternoon lessons, with school ending at 4:30 P.M. The majority of children have lunch at school, but each family can decide whether their children stay at school or go home for 2 hours. In state elementary school, children have to pay only for the meals they consume in schools.

When parents need extra time in school for child care because of their work schedule, they can apply to have children in school an hour earlier (at 7:30 A.M.). Some schools also offer activities for 2 hours after school (until 6:30 P.M.). In the morning, support staff looks after the children, and in the afternoon the children can practice sports, music, theatre, or other activities with specialized nonteaching personnel. The cost for the morning extra time is 70 Euro per year; for the afternoon time the parents pay a small amount for the specific activities they select for their children.

Each class has two teachers who stay with the same class for 5 years. They teach all the subjects except English as a second language (starting generally in third grade) and Catholic religion which are taught by other teachers. Those families who do not want their children to attend religion class can apply for other types of alternative activities.

As for training, elementary school teachers normally have 4-year *istituti magistrali* diplomas (these are equivalent to American high school diplomas with a specialty in education), and then have to pass a test to practice. They also have the first year of practice or student teaching as part of their training. As in the case of preschool teachers, beginning in 1998 all future elementary school teachers have to attend 4 years of university as part of their training.

In 1996 teachers earned about 1,100 Euro per month (13 months per year counting the Christmas month bonus) after taxes, with all the benefits accorded to state employees in Italy. Their working schedule is 24 hours a week, 22 of which are spent in the class, and 2 in planning and meetings. Many teachers, of course, spend a good deal of time outside the classroom preparing lessons and evaluating students' work.

After the 1999 law on school autonomy, each school can decide to use part of its funds to pay teachers for extra work that can be spent on special projects. In the school where we collected data, for example, some teachers were paid (about 25 Euro per hour before taxes) to work with children who had learning difficulties, while other teachers organized some activities with foreign children to help with Italian comprehension and production.

Educational Philosophy

It is very difficult to trace general educational objectives of the *scuola elementare*, given that it is not a local institution, as was the case of the *scuola dell'infanzia*. We can therefore only highlight some very general features of the state elementary school in Italy:

- School is free and accepts all children, of any nationality.
- Children with special needs have the right to attend regular classes and follow programs that are based on their needs.
- School guarantees that all children with learning difficulties can follow programs particularly aimed to address their needs.
- All children in school have the right to reach a minimum level of abilities.

The educational philosophy of *scuole elementari* on a local level is best discerned in the special projects it implements. In the Emilia-Romagna region, and most particularly in Modena, several specific projects have been widely supported.

- For example, since the early 1990s schools have the possibility of assigning some teachers to specific programs through a year long contract. In other words, some teachers can apply to assume roles other than that of teachers, without any change in their salary or weekly working schedule. This opportunity has been widely used by the schools in Modena, most of which assign a teacher to plan activities for children with special needs, or coordinate the various activities in the school, or work specifically to aid the integration of foreign children into the school.
- Another project in recent years that all the schools in Modena agreed to work on is aimed at the early identification of difficulties in reading and writing (e.g., dyslexia). The teachers now screen all children at the begin-

ning of each year (with particular attention to first- and second-year classes) with standardized reading tests, and then give a second round of tests a few months later.

- Modena has also made an important investment in terms of resources in a project directed at the prevention of social problems through health education. Experts often come to the schools to talk to the children and discuss how they behave in different situations and what they can do to live healthier lives, both physically and psychologically.

- Finally, as in the *scuole dell'infanzia*, the relationship between the school and the community is strongly encouraged. The local government offers several opportunities each year for visits to exhibitions or monuments. Other activities involve larger projects of solidarity. For example, before Christmas the children are invited to draw pictures or to write texts and poems to bring to their peers who are in the hospital. In some schools, children are invited to give up snacks in school for a certain period of time and instead give one Euro to fund a volunteer organization supporting children's needs.

References

Abbot, A. (1992). What do cases do? Some notes on activity in sociological analysis. In C. Ragin & H. Becker (Eds.), *What is a case: Exploring the foundations of social inquiry* (pp. 53–82). New York: Cambridge University Press.

Adler, P. A., & Adler, P. (1998). *Peer power: Preadolescent culture and identity.* New Brunswick, NJ: Rutgers University Press.

Alexander, K., & Entwisle, D. (1988). *Achievement in the first 2 years of school: Patterns and processes.* Monographs of the Society for Research in Child Development, vol. 53, no. 2 (serial no. 218). Chicago: University of Chicago Press.

Alexander, K., Entwisle, D., & Horsey, C. (1997). From first grade forward: Early foundations of high school dropout. *Sociology of Education, 70,* 87–107.

Aydt, H., & Corsaro, W. (2003). Differences in children's construction of gender across culture: An interpretive approach. *American Behavioral Scientist, 46,* 1306–1325.

Baldisserri, M. M. (1980). *Scuola materna, scuola dell'infanzia.* Firenze: La Nuova Italia.

Ball, S. (1980). Initial encounters in the classroom and the process of establishment. In P. Woods (Ed.), *Pupil strategies: Explorations in the sociology of the school* (pp. 143–161). London: Croom Helm.

Barnett, W. S. (1996). Long-term effects of early childhood programs on cognitive and school outcomes. *The Future of Children, 5*(3), 25–50.

Berentzen, S. (1984). *Children constructing their social world.* Bergen Studies in Social Anthropology, no. 36. Bergen, Norway: Department of Social Anthropology, University of Bergen.

Berentzen, S. (1995). *Boyfriend-girlfriend relationships in social organization: A study of the growth and decline of "go-with" relationships in a black ghetto.* Unpublished manuscript.

Bergmann, B. R. (1996). *Saving our children from poverty: What the United States can learn from France.* New York: Russell Sage Foundation.

Bertolini, P. (1984). *L'infanzia e la sua scuola.* Firenze: La Nuova Italia.

Blau, D., & Mocan, H. (2002). The supply of quality in child care centers. *Review of Economics and Statistics, 84*(3), 483–496.

Bourdieu, P. (1977). *Outline of a theory of practice.* New York: Cambridge University Press.

Brauner, J., Gordic, B., & Zigler, E. (2004). Putting the child back into child care: Combining care and education for children ages 3–5. *Social Policy Report, 18*(3), 3–15.

Bronfenbrenner, U. (1979). *The ecology of human development: Experiments by nature and design*. Cambridge, MA: Harvard University Press.

Bronfenbrenner, U., & Morris, P. A. (1998). The ecology of developmental processes. In W. Damon & R. Lerner (Eds.), *Handbook of child psychology* (Vol. 1, pp. 993–1028). New York: Wiley.

Bruner, J. (1986). *Actual minds, possible worlds*. Cambridge, MA: Harvard University Press.

Cadwell, L. (1997). *Bringing Reggio Emilia home: An innovative approach to early childhood education*. New York: Teachers College Press.

Cadwell, L (2003). *Bringing learning to life: The Reggio approach to early childhood education*. New York: Teachers College Press.

Ciari, B. (1961). *Le nuove tecniche didattiche*. Rome: Editori Riuniti.

Ciari, B. (1972). *La grande disadattata*. Rome: Editori Riuniti.

Consortium of Longitudinal Studies. (Ed.). (1983). *As the twig is bent: Lasting effects of preschool programs*. Mahwah, NJ: Lawrence Erlbaum.

Corsaro, W. A. (1985). *Friendship and peer culture in the early years*. Norwood, NJ: Ablex.

Corsaro, W. A. (1992). Interpretive reproduction in children's peer cultures. *Social Psychology Quarterly, 55*, 160–177.

Corsaro, W. A. (1993). Interpretive reproduction in children's role play. *Childhood, 1*, 64–74.

Corsaro, W. A. (1994). Discussion, debate and friendship: Peer discourse in nursery schools in the United States and Italy. *Sociology of Education, 67*, 1–26.

Corsaro, W. A. (1996). Transitions in early childhood: The promise of comparative, longitudinal ethnography. In R. Jessor, A. Colby, & R. Shweder (Eds.), *Ethnography and human development: Context and meaning in social inquiry* (pp. 419–458). Chicago: University of Chicago Press.

Corsaro, W. A. (2003). *"We're friends, right?": Inside kids' culture*. Washington, DC: Joseph Henry Press.

Corsaro, W. A. (2005). *The sociology of childhood* (2nd ed.). Thousand Oaks, CA: Pine Forge Press.

Corsaro, W. A., & Emiliani, F. (1992). Child care, early education, and children's peer culture in Italy. In M. Lamb, K. Sternberg, C. Hwang, & A. Broberg (Eds.), *Child care in context: Cross-cultural perspectives* (pp. 81–115). Hillsdale, NJ: Lawrence Erlbaum.

Corsaro, W. A., & Miller P. (Eds.). (1992). *Interpretive approaches to children's socialization*. New Directions in Child Development, no. 58. San Francisco: Jossey-Bass.

Corsaro, W. A., & Molinari, L. (1990). From *seggiolini* to *discussione*: The generation and extension of peer culture among Italian preschool children. *International Journal of Qualitative Studies in Education, 3*, 213–230.

Corsaro, W. A., & Molinari, L. (2000a). Entering and observing in children's worlds: A reflection on a longitudinal ethnography of early education in Italy. In P. Christensen & A. James (Eds.), *Research with children: Perspectives and practices* (pp. 179–200). London: Falmer Press.

Corsaro, W. A., & Molinari, L. (2000b). Priming events and Italian children's transition from preschool to elementary school: Representations and action. *Social Psychology Quarterly, 63,* 16–33.

Corsaro, W. A., Molinari, L., Hadley, K., & Sugioka, H. (2003). Keeping and making friends in Italian children's transition from preschool to elementary school. *Social Psychology Quarterly, 66,* 272–292.

Corsaro, W. A., Molinari, L., & Rosier, K. B. (2002). Zena and Carlotta: Transition narratives and early education in the United States and Italy. *Human Development, 45,* 323–348.

Corsaro, W. A., & Nelson, E. (2003). Children's collective activities and peer culture in early literacy in American and Italian preschools. *Sociology of Education, 76,* 209–227.

Corsaro, W. A., & Rizzo, T. A. (1988). *Discussione* and friendship: Socialization processes in the peer culture of Italian nursery school children. *American Sociological Review, 53,* 879–894.

Corsaro, W. A., & Rosier, K. B. (2002). Priming events, autonomy, and agency in low-income African-American children's transition from home to school. In R. Edwards (Ed.), *Children, home, and school: Regulation, autonomy or connection* (pp. 136–154). London: RoutledgeFalmer.

Della Sala, V. (2002). "Modernization" and welfare-state restructuring in Italy: The impact on child care. In S. Michel & R. Mahon (Eds.), *Child care policy at the crossroads: Gender and welfare state restructuring* (pp. 171–189). New York: Routledge.

Delpit, L. (1992). Education in a multicultural society: Our future's greatest challenge. *Journal of Negro Education, 61,* 237–249.

Duveen, G., & Lloyd, B. (Eds.). (1990). *Social representations and the development of knowledge.* Cambridge, UK: Cambridge University Press.

Edwards, C. (1998). Partner, nurturer, and guide: The role of the teacher. In C. Edwards, L. Gandini, & G. Forman (Eds.), *The hundred languages of children: The Reggio Emilia approach—advanced reflections* (pp. 179–198). Greenwich, CT: Ablex.

Edwards, C. P., Gandini, L., & Forman, G. (Eds.). (1993). *The hundred languages of children: The Reggio Emilia approach.* Greenwich, CT: Ablex.

Edwards, C. P., Gandini, L., & Forman, G. (Eds.). (1998). *The hundred languages of children: The Reggio Emilia approach—advanced reflections.* Greenwich, CT: Ablex.

Elder, G. H., Jr. (1974). *Children of the great depression: Social change in life experience.* Chicago: University of Chicago Press.

Elder, G. H., Jr. (1994). Time, human agency, and social change: Perspectives of the live course. *Social Psychology Quarterly, 57,* 4–15.

Emirbayer, M., & Mische, A. (1998). What is agency? *American Journal of Sociology, 103,* 962–1023.

Entwisle, D. (1995). The role of schools in sustaining benefits of early childhood programs. *The Future of Childhood, 5,* 133–144.

Entwisle, D. R., & Alexander, K. L. (1999). Early schooling and social stratification. In R. C. Pianta & M. J. Cox (Eds.), *The transition to kindergarten* (pp. 13–38). Baltimore, MD: P. H. Brookes.

Entwisle, D., & Alexander, K., & Olson, L. (1997). *Children, schools and inequality*. New York: Westview.

Evaldsson, A. C. (1993). *Play, disputes and social order: Everyday life in two Swedish after-school centers*. Linköping, Sweden: Linköping University.

Evaldsson, A. C., & Corsaro, W. A. (1998). Play and games in the peer cultures of preschool and preadolescent children. *Childhood, 5,* 377–402.

Fagot, B. (1994). Peer relations and the development of competence in boys and girls. *New Directions for Child Development, 65,* 53–65.

Fernie, D., Kantor, R., & Whaley, K. (1995). Learning from classroom ethnographies: Same places, different times. In A. Hatch (Ed.), *Qualitative research in early education settings* (pp. 155–172). Westport, CT: Greenwood.

Flaherty, M. (1984). A formal approach to the study of amusement in social interaction. *Studies in Symbolic Interaction, 5,* 71–82.

Flyvbjerg, B. (2004). Five misunderstandings about case-study research. In C. Seale, G. Gobo, J. Gubrium, & D. Silverman (Eds.), *Qualitative research practice* (pp. 420–434). London: Sage.

Frabboni, F. (1984). Dagli orientamenti al curricolo: Passaggio pedagogico obbligato per la scuola dell'infanzia. In P. Bertolini (Ed.), *La scuola dell'infanzia verso il 2000* (pp. 71–83). Firenze: La Nuova Italia.

Furstenberg, F., Cook, T. D., Eccles, J., & Elder, G. (2000). *Managing to make it: Urban families and adolescent success*. Chicago: University of Chicago Press.

Gandini, L., & Edwards, C. P. (Eds.). (2001). *Bambini: The Italian approach to infant/toddler care*. New York: Teachers College Press.

Gandini, L, Hill, L., Cadwell, L., & Schwall, C. (Eds.). (2005). *In the spirit of the studio: Learning from the atelier of Reggio Emilia*. New York: Teachers College Press.

Geertz, C. (1973). *The interpretation of cultures*. New York: Basic Books.

Geertz, C. (1983). *Local knowledge: Further essays in interpretive anthropology*. New York: Basic Books.

Giddens, A. (1991). *Modernity and self-identity*. Stanford, CA: Stanford University Press.

Giudici, C., Rinaldi, C., & Krechevsky, M. (Eds.). (2001). *Making learning visible: Children as individual and group learners*. Reggio Emilia, Italy: Reggio Children.

Goffman, E. (1961). *Asylums*. Garden City, NJ: Anchor.

Goffman, E. (1974). *Frame analysis*. New York: Harper & Row.

Goodwin, M. H. (1998). Games of stance: Conflict and footing in hopscotch. In S. Hoyle & C. D. Adger (Eds.), *Kids' talk: Strategic language use in later childhood* (pp. 23–46). New York: Oxford University Press.

Goodwin, M. H. (2003). The relevance of ethnicity, class, and gender in children's peer negotiation. In J. Holmes & M. Meyerhoff (Eds.), *Handbook of language and gender* (pp. 229–251). New York: Blackwell.

Gormley, W., & Phillips, D. (2003). *The effects of universal pre-K in Oklahoma: Research highlights and policy implications*. Retrieved from: http://www.crocus. georgetown.edu/working.paper.2.pdf

Gottman, J. (1986). The world of coordinated play: Same- and cross-sex friendships in young children. In J. Gottman & S. Parker (Eds.), *Conversations among friends: Speculations on affective development*. New York: Cambridge University Press.

Graue, E. (1999). Integrating diverse perspectives on kindergarten contexts and practice. In R. C. Pianta & M. Cox (Eds.), *The transition to kindergarten* (pp. 109–143). Baltimore, MD: P. H. Brookes.

Heath, S. B. (1983). *Ways with words: Language, life, and work in communities and classrooms*. New York: Cambridge University Press.

Helburn, S., & Bergmann, B. (2002). *America's child care problem*. New York: Palgrave.

Hellman, S. (1987). Italy. In M. Kesselman & J. Krieger (Eds.), *European politics in transition* (pp. 320–450). Lexington, MA: D. G. Heath.

Helm, J., & Katz, L. (2001). *Young investigators: The project approach in the early years*. New York: Teachers College Press.

Jacobson, L. (1997). "Looping" catches on as a way to build strong ties. *Education Week, 17*(1), 18–19.

James, A., Jenks, C., & Prout, A. (1998). *Theorizing childhood*. New York: Teachers College Press.

Kamerman, S. (2000). Early childhood intervention policies: An international perspective. In J. Shonkoff & S. Meisels (Eds.), *Handbook of early childhood intervention* (2nd ed., pp. 613–629). New York: Cambridge University Press.

Katz, L. (1998). What can we learn from Reggio Emilia? In C. Edwards, L. Gandini, & G. Forman (Eds.), *The hundred languages of children: The Reggio Emilia approach—advanced reflections* (pp. 27–45). Greenwich, CT: Ablex.

Kimball, S. (1960). Introduction. In A. van Gennep, *The rites of passage*. Chicago: University of Chicago Press.

Kyratzis, A. (2001). Children's gender indexing in language: From the separate world hypothesis to considerations of culture, context, and power. *Research on Language and Social Interaction, 34*, 1–13.

Ladd, G., & Price, G. (1987). Predicting children's social and school adjustment following the transition from preschool to kindergarten. *Child Development, 58*, 1168–1189.

LaFreniere, P., Strayer, F., & Gauthier, R. (1984). The emergence of same-sex affiliative preferences among preschool peers: A developmental/ethological perspective. *Child Development, 55*, 1958–1965.

Lamb, M., Sternberg, K., Hwang, C., & Broberg, A. (Eds.). (1992). *Child care in context: Cross-cultural perspectives*. Hillsdale, NJ: Lawrence Erlbaum.

Lave, G., & Wenger, E. (1991). *Situated learning: Legitimate peripheral participation*. New York: Cambridge University Press.

Maccoby, E. E. (1999). *The two sexes: Growing up apart, coming together*. Cambridge, MA: Harvard University Press.

Maccoby, E. E., & Jacklin, C. N. (1987). Gender segregation in childhood. In E. Reese (Ed.), *Advances in child development and behavior* (Vol. 20, pp. 239–287). New York: Academic Press.

Maccoby, E. E., & Lewis C. (2003). Less day care or different day care? *Human Development, 74,* 1069–1075.

Malaguzzi, L. (1998). History, ideas, and basic philosophy: An interview with Lella Gandini. In C. P. Edwards, L. Gandini, & G. Forman (Eds.), *The hundred languages of children: The Reggio Emilia approach—advanced reflections* (pp. 49–98). Greenwich, CT: Ablex.

Manini, M. (1984). La scuola dell'infanzia dagli orientamenti al curricolo: Motivazioni socioeducative e considerazioni operative. In P. Bertolini (Ed.), *La scuola dell'infanzia verso il 2000* (pp. 106–121). Firenze: La Nuova Italia.

Mantovani, S. (1998). *Nostalgia del futuro.* Lama San Giustino (PG), Italy: Edizioni Junior.

Mayall, B. (2002). *Towards a sociology for childhood: Thinking from children's lives.* Philadelphia, PA: Open University Press.

Mead, G. H. (1934). *Mind, self, and society.* Chicago: University of Chicago Press.

Merton, R. (1968). *Social theory and social structure.* New York: Free Press.

Mishler, E. (1979). "Won't you trade cookies with the popcorn": The talk of trades among six-year-olds. In O. Garnica & M. King (Eds.), *Language, children and society: The effects of social factors on children's learning to communicate* (pp. 21–36). Elmsford, NY: Pergamon.

Molinari, L., & Corsaro, W. A. (1994). La gnesi el'evoluzione della cultura dei bambini. *Bambini, 10,* 38–45.

Mosier, C., & Rogoff, B. (1995). *Cultural variation in young children's roles in the family: Autonomy and responsibility.* Unpublished manuscript.

Mozère, L. (1984). Bisogni degli utenti e intervento dello Stato. Dinamica istituzionale e amministrativa: il caso dei nidi d'infanzia in Francia. In P. Ghedini (Ed.), *Quali prospettive per l'infanzia: Partecipazione e gestione dei servizi nella trasformazione dello stato sociale* (pp. 41–50). Firenze: La Nuova Italia.

National Institute of Child Health and Human Development (NICHD) Early Child Care Research Network. (2003). Does amount of time spent in child care predict socioemotional adjustment during the transition to kindergarten? *Child Development, 74,* 976–1005.

Neri, S. (2001). *Guardare vicino e lontano.* Milano: Fabbri Editori.

New, R. (1997). Next steps in teaching "The Reggio Way": Advocating for a new image of the child. In J. Hendrick (Ed.), *First steps in teaching the Reggio way* (pp. 224–233). Columbus, OH: Merrill.

New, R. (2001). Early literacy and developmentally appropriate practice: Rethinking the paradigm. In S. B. Neuman & D. K. Dickinson (Eds.), *Handbook of early literacy research* (pp. 245–260). New York: Guilford Press.

O'Mara-Thieman, J. (2003). The water to river project. In J. H. Helm & S. Beneke (Eds.), *The power of projects* (pp. 42–49). New York: Teachers College Press.

Orsolini, M., & Pontecorvo, C. (1992). Children's talk in classroom discussions. *Cognition and Instruction, 9,* 113–136.

Parsons, T., & Bales, R. (1955). *Family, socialization, and interaction process.* New York: Free Press.

Piaget, J. (1950). *The psychology of intelligence.* London: Routledge & Kegan Paul.

Pianta, R., & Cox, M. (1999a). The changing nature of the transition to school: Trends for the next decade. In R. Pianta & M. Cox (Eds.), *The transition to kindergarten* (pp. 363–379). Baltimore, MD: Brookes Publishing.

Pianta, R., & Cox, M. (Eds.). (1999b). *The transition to kindergarten*. Baltimore, MD: Brookes Publishing.

Pianta, R., & Walsh, D. (1996). *High-risk children in schools: Constructing sustaining relationships*. New York: Routledge.

Pistillo, F. (1989). Preprimary education and care in Italy. In P. Olmsted & D. Weikart (Eds.), *How nations serve young children: Profiles of child care and education in 14 countries* (pp. 151–202). Ypsilanti, MI: The High/Scope Press.

Pontecorvo, C., Fasulo, A., & Sterponi, L. (2001). Mutual apprentices: The making of parenthood and childhood in family dinner conversations. *Human Development, 44*, 340–361.

Putnam, R. D. (1993). *Making democracy work: Civic traditions in modern Italy*. Princeton, NJ: Princeton University Press.

Putnam, R. D. (1996). The strange disappearance of civic America. *The American Prospect, 24*, 344–350.

Raden, A. (1999). *Universal prekindergarten in Georgia: A case study of Georgia's lottery-funded pre-K program*. Working Paper Series. New York: Foundation for Child Development. Retrieved February 15, 2005, from http://www.fcd-us.org/news/publications-wip.html

Ramsey, P. (1991). *Making friends in school: Promoting peer relationships in early childhood*. New York: Teachers College Press.

Rapporto della commissione per la revisione degli orientamenti per la scuola materna. (1989).

Rimm-Kaufman, S., & Pianta, R. (2000). An ecological perspective on the transition to kindergarten: A theoretical framework to guide empirical research. *Journal of Applied Developmental Psychology, 21*, 491–511.

Rizzo, T. A. (1989). *Friendship development among children in school*. Norwood, NJ: Ablex.

Rizzo, T. A., Corsaro, W. A., & Bates, J. E. (1992). Ethnographic methods and interpretive analysis: Expanding the methodological options of psychologists. *Developmental Review, 12*, 101–123.

Rogoff, B. (1995). Observing sociocultural activity on three planes: Participatory appropriation, guided participation, and apprenticeship. In J. Wertsch, P. Del Rio, & A. Alvarez (Eds.), *Sociocultural studies of mind* (pp. 139–164). New York: Cambridge University Press.

Rogoff, B. (1996). Developmental transitions in children's participation in sociocultural activities. In A. Sameroff & M. Haith (Eds.), *The Five to Seven Year Shift* (pp. 273–294). Chicago: University of Chicago Press

Rogoff, B. (2003). *The cultural nature of human development*. New York: Oxford.

Rogoff, B., Baker-Sennett, J., & Matusov, E. (1994). Considering the concept of planning. In M. Haith, J. Benson, R. Roberts, & B. Pennington (Eds.), *The development of future-oriented processes* (pp. 353–373). Chicago: University of Chicago Press.

Rosier, K. B. (2000). *Mothering inner-city children: The early school years.* New Brunswick, NJ: Rutgers University Press.

Schatzman, L., & Strauss, A. (1973). *Field research: Strategies for natural sociology.* Englewood Cliffs, NJ: Prentice-Hall.

Tesson, G., & Youniss, J. (1995). Micro-sociology and psychological development: A sociological interpretation of Piaget's theory. *Sociological Studies of Children and Youth, 7,* 101–126.

Thelen, E., & Smith, L. (1998). Dynamic systems theory. In R. Lerner (Ed.), *Handbook of child psychology* (pp. 563–634). New York: Wiley.

Thorne, B. (1993). *Gender play: Girls and boys in school.* New Brunswick, NJ: Rutgers University Press.

Tobin, J., Wu, F., & Davidson, D. (1991). *Preschool in three cultures.* New Haven, CT: Yale University Press.

Turner, V. (1974). *Drama, fields, and metaphors: Symbolic action in human society.* Ithaca, NY: Cornell University Press.

U.S. Office of Management and Budget. (2005). *Budget of the United States government: Fiscal year 2005.* Retrieved January 10, 2005, from http://www.gpoaccess.gov/usbudget/fy05/browse.html

van Gennep, A. (1960). *The rites of passage.* Chicago: University of Chicago Press.

Vecchi, V. (1998). The role of the *atelierista*; An interview with Lella Gandini. In C. P. Edwards, L. Gandini, & G. Forman (Eds.), *The hundred languages of children: The Reggio Emilia approach—advanced reflections* (pp. 139–147). Greenwich, CT: Ablex.

Vecchiotti, S. (2003). Kindergarten: An overlooked educational policy priority. *Social Policy Report, 17*(2), 3–19.

Vygotsky, L. (1978). *Mind in society.* Cambridge, MA: Harvard University Press.

Wertsch, J. (1998). *Mind as action.* New York: Oxford University Press.

Wulff, H. (1988). *Twenty girls: Growing up, ethnicity, and excitement in a South London microculture.* Stockholm: University of Stockholm.

Index

189

About the Authors

William A. Corsaro is the Robert H. Shaffer Class of 1967 Endowed Professor of Sociology at Indiana University, Bloomington. He received his Ph.D. in sociology from the University of North Carolina, Chapel Hill. Corsaro was a Fulbright Senior Research Fellow in Bologna, Italy, in 1983–84 and a Fulbright Senior Specialist Fellow in Trondheim, Norway, in 2003. Among his writings are *Friendship and Peer Culture in the Early Years* (1985), *"We're Friends, Right?": Inside Kids' Culture* (2003), and *The Sociology of Childhood* (2nd ed. 2005). His research interests include the sociology of childhood, children's peer cultures, and early education from a comparative perspective.

Luisa Molinari is Professor of Developmental Psychology at the University of Parma, Italy. She received her Ph.D. in psychology from the University of Bologna, Italy. Her writings include *Psicologia dello Sviluppo Sociale* (2002), *Rappresentazioni e Affetti* (coauthored with Francesca Emiliani, 1995), and *Il Bambino nella Mente e nelle Parole delle Madri* (coauthored with Francesca Emiliani, 1989). Her main research interests concern the socialization processes of children in the family and the school, and parents' social representations of children's development and education.